To My Mother And Father, who showed me all the right paths and let me explore them on my own, and to Judy, Starsky, and Harry-O, who came along on a lot of them.

Where to Walk Your Dog
in
SANTA CLARA and
SAN MATEO COUNTIES

Cheryl Smith

WILDERNESS PRESS
BERKELEY

Copyright © 1991 by Cheryl S. Smith
Photos and maps by the author
Drawings by Jon Larson
Design by Thomas Winnett
Cover design by Larry Van Dyke and Jane Brundage

Library of Congress Catalog Number 91-20620
ISBN 0-89997-120-2

Manufactured in the United States of America
Published by Wilderness Press
                2440 Bancroft Way
                Berkeley, CA 94704
                (415) 843-8080

        Write or call for free catalog

♻ Printed on recycled paper

Library of Congress Cataloging-in-Publication Data
Smith, Cheryl S.
      Where to walk your dog in Santa Clara and San Mateo counties /
Cheryl S. Smith. — 1st ed.
            p. cm.
      Includes index.
      ISBN 0-89997-127-X
1. Dog walking—California—Santa Clara County—Guide-books. 2. Dog
walking—California—San Mateo County—Guide-books. 3. Santa Clara
County (Calif.)—Description and travel—Guide-books. 4. San Mateo
County
(Calif.)—Description and travel—Guide-books.
I. Title.
SF 427.46.s65 1991
636.7—dc20   91-20620
                                                  CIP

Contents

Part 2: The Rest of Santa Clara County
Chapter 1: Milpitas

Chapter 2: Santa Clara

Chapter 3: Campbell

Chapter 4: Los Gatos

Chapter 5: Saratoga

Chapter 6: Cupertino

Chapter 7: Sunnyvale

Introduction

The Bay Area is blessed with an excellent park system, from the city level, through county and regional organizations, to the state and national level. But as most dog owners are aware, a great number of these parks refuse admittance to dogs. no matter how well-behaved, or allow them only in certain campgrounds or picnic areas. With so many different regulatory bodies, finding out where you're welcome can be time-consuming and frustrating.

I hope this series of books will solve that problem. I have included every place of reasonable size I could find where you can walk with your dog, from tiny city parks encircled by busy streets to large tracts of wilderness where it's actually legal to let your dog run free. You will also find information on any local government regulations directly relating to dogs.

This book covers Santa Clara County, divided into San Jose and the rest of the county, and San Mateo County. Other books will cover Alameda and Contra Costa, and San Francisco and Marin. I have tried to be thorough, but it's a large area and obviously some parts of it are more familiar to me than others. If I have missed one of your favorite spots, please let me know for future editions. You can write to me care of the publisher. Do keep in mind, however, that only areas where dogs are legally welcomed are included.

While on the subject of welcome, let me plead with all of you to be responsible dog owners. If park rules state that your dog must be kept on a six-foot leash, please comply. While you may think that your four-footed friend is pining for his freedom, he's probably delighted just to be walking with you. Our dogs appreciate the time we spend with them. If that time also provides them with the chance to investigate a variety of settings, so much the better.

Of course, the other main responsibility of people walking their dogs is to clean up after them. None of us finds this particularly pleasant, but neglecting it can lead to more No Dogs Allowed signs. If you don't want to be burdened with a pooper-scooper, a few sandwich bags stuffed in a pocket will prove serviceable. Be considerate of other park users. Don't trip joggers with your leash or cause a disturbance with your dog's barking. Don't let your pet run up to strangers—they may be afraid of dogs. Even other dog owners may not appreciate your approaching too closely—not all dogs are friendly toward strange canines. If we all behave well and demonstrate that our dogs do not have a detrimental effect on parklands, perhaps more will open up to us. At least it will make it easier for the pro-dog interest groups that are springing up to press their point.

For those who might be interested in such groups, or in training clubs or other dog-related organizations, there is a Resources section at the back of the book. I do recommend at least basic obedience training. It makes a better citizen of your dog and a better handler of you.

You will also find a list of parks of special interest at the end of the book—places where you can really have a walk or find something of historical interest, and places you might want to visit for some other reason.

All the maps in this book are meant to be general indicators of park location. They include mostly main routes and whatever smaller roads are necessary to get to a park. The roads mentioned in the "Locations" section of the park listings are not necessarily shown on the maps. In all cases, consult a bona-fide road map before attempting to reach any park with which you are not familiar.

I hope you will find this guide useful, and that it will inspire you to take your dog for a visit to many of the fine parks listed herein. My own dogs undoubtedly wish the research had gone on forever.

Cheryl S. Smith,
Spirit and Serling,
and Sundance, who will
always be with us

Part One
Santa Clara County: San Jose

Santa Clara County covers an area of 1,316 square miles. Much of that space seems to be occupied by sprawling San Jose. And all of San Jose is liberally sprinkled with city parks of varying sizes and amenities.

San Jose has a pleasantly benevolent attitude toward dogs. With just a few exceptions (noted at the end of this part) dogs are allowed in all city parks. There are three pertinent city ordinances:

708.200 Animals Running at Large

708.412 Public Nuisance—Dog Droppings

708.590 Restraint of Dogs

What they amount to, in effect, are a leash law and a pooper-scooper law. You are expected to keep your pet on a six-foot leash (these are not wilderness areas, after all) and to clean up after yourselves.

Except for a few group areas, the picnic tables and barbecues are available on a first-come first-served basis. If you are interested in any special facilities, such as bocce-ball courts or lawn bowling, check with the San Jose Parks and Recreation Department (277-5351) for availability and regulations.

Because San Jose *is* such a large, sprawling city, this chapter breaks it into sections, with a map preceding each section. The maps are meant as general indicators of location. Consult a local street map before setting out to visit a park in an unfamiliar area.

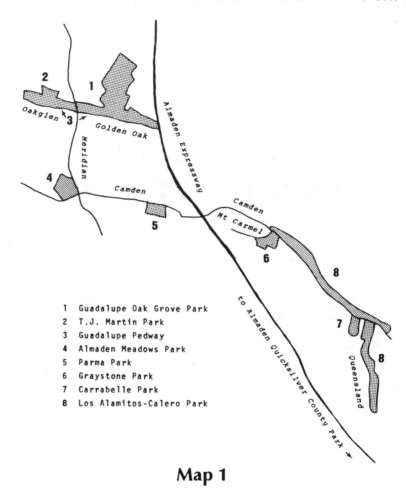

1 Guadalupe Oak Grove Park
2 T.J. Martin Park
3 Guadalupe Pedway
4 Almaden Meadows Park
5 Parma Park
6 Graystone Park
7 Carrabelle Park
8 Los Alamitos-Calero Park

Map 1

Walk 1: Guadalupe Oak Grove Park

Location: Golden Oak Way off Meridian Avenue or Vargas Drive off Coleman Road—easy to find. See Map 1.

Size: 56 acres, all open natural vegetation

Parking: Small lot on Thorntree, street parking on Vargas and Golden Oak

For Comfort: Restrooms, with wheelchair access, sparkling clean, near parking lot; water fountain at same location

Description: Section at Vargas entrance is hilly, but main path winds between hills. Back section off Golden Oak is flat. Vargas side is more open, with scattered oaks on the hillsides. Back section is an actual oak grove, quiet and full of dappled shade. New trees are being planted to replace those that have fallen. Dirt paths wind through the grove and up and over the hills.

Of Note: This is a positively gorgeous park, where I have been alone each time I have visited. Lots of birds, including some attractive flickers. A good place to wander and let your thoughts do likewise.

Walk 2: T. J. Martin Park

Location: The Strand off Burchell Avenue off Meridian Avenue—easy to find. See Map 1.

Size: 23.60 acres, nearly all open grass, and including this section of the Guadalupe Pedway

Parking: Neighborhood street parking

For Comfort: Water fountain

For Sports: 3 chess tables

For Kids: Playground

Description: Slightly rolling, with good grass. Not much shade. Paved path across park, connecting with section of Guadalupe Pedway. Has lights and benches, and powerlines above.

Of Note: The park is a good point of entry for this section of the Guadalupe Pedway.

Walk 3: Guadalupe Pedway Parcels

Location: Golden Oak Way and Oakglen Way off Meridian Avenue—easy to find. See Map 1.

Size: 19.99 acres, mostly open grass

Parking: Neighborhood street parking

For Comfort: Water fountain

For Sports: Parcourse

For Kids: Playground

Description: Mostly flat area under high powerlines that has been planted in grass and has some landscaping. Long and narrow, running between Almaden Expressway and Coleman Road. Paved path with lights running down length. Dirt path with parcourse running mostly along Oakglen section. Golden Oaks Park is currently under construction at the east end to complete the section between McAbee and Almaden.

Of Note: There are lots of joggers and people walking their dogs—most of them on leash. You can enter the back of Guadalupe Oak Grove Park from the pedway in the Golden Oak section.

Walk 4: Almaden Meadows Park

Location: Camden Avenue between Skyfarm Drive and Meridian Avenue—on main road, easy to find. See Map 1.

Size: 15.50 acres, mostly open grass or natural areas

Parking: Street parking

For Comfort: Water fountain

For Dining: 8 picnic tables, 4 barbecues

For Kids: Playground

Description: Other than the playground and picnic tables, in an undeveloped state. Large hill covers about half the park, with dirt trails leading up. Can be muddy. Poison oak in natural areas. Broken glass on some parts of hill. Grass and plants on lower section very lush.

Of Note: You can enjoy a nice short burst of mountain climbing on the hill and be finished before you have a chance to really lose your breath. There is a pleasant flat area on top, with live oaks offering shade.

Walk 5: Parma Park

Location: Camden Avenue between Little Falls Drive and Grapevine Way—on main road, easy to find. See Map 1.

Size: 4.78 acres, half open grass

Parking: Neighborhood street parking

For Comfort: Water fountain

For Sports: Playing field at adjacent school

For Dining: 15 tables, 6 barbecues

For Kids: 2 playgrounds

Description: Slightly hilly, grass except for dirt areas around picnic tables and playgrounds. Very little shade. Unfenced. Backs on very active school yard.

Of Note: This is a very high-usage park, and unless you have a social dog and you both enjoy meeting people, I wouldn't recommend it.

Walk 6: Graystone Park

Location: Camden Avenue between Mt. Carmel Drive and Valentine Drive—on main road, easy to find. See Map 1.

Size: 4.73 acres, about two-thirds open grass

Parking: Neighborhood street parking

For Comfort: Water fountain

For Sports: Ballfield at adjacent school

For Dining: 6 tables, 3 barbecues

For Kids: Playground, bike racks

Description: Slightly hilly, nice soft grass. Paved path to and around both playgrounds, with lights. Lots of beautiful big shade trees. Unfenced.

Of Note: A good park for a rainy day. The rain might cut down on the normally high usage, and the trees offer plenty of cover.

Walk 7: Carrabelle Park

Location: Camden Avenue between Shearwater Drive and Villagewood Way—on main road, easy to find. See Map 1.

Size: 2.86 acres, about three-quarters open grass

Parking: Neighborhood street parking

For Comfort: Water fountain

For Dining: 8 picnic tables

For Kids: Playground, bike racks

Description: Rolling terrain, lush grass. Good paved path winding along three sides of the park, with lights. Unfenced.

Of Note: This makes a good lunch stop if you're walking the Los Alamitos-Calero Park Chain trail.

Walk 8: Los Alamitos-Calero Park Chain

Location: Final stretch of Camden Avenue, length of Queenswood Way—on main road, easy to find. See Map 1.

Size: 13.61 acres, mostly linear

Parking: Neighborhood street parking, not allowed on Camden

Description: Paved trail along top of levee above creek, dirt and gravel trail closer to creek on some stretches. Dirt trail along far side of creek for length of Queenswood. Lots of shade areas. Used by bicyclists and equestrians also.

Of Note: This is a great bona-fide trail, especially long if you have no one to bring the car around and have to walk both ways. You can stay clean and dry on the main path, risk some burrs on the creek path, or get wet in the creek. There was water only in the Camden section on my visit. I was also warned of a flasher by some local walkers. You can find drinking water and picnic tables in Graystone and Carrabelle Parks, located across the street from different sections of the trail.

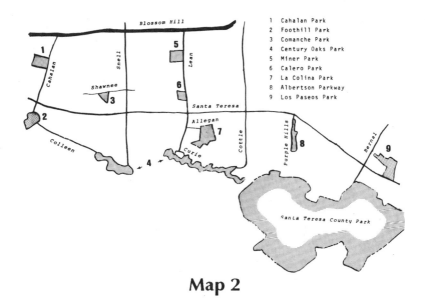

1 Cahalan Park
2 Foothill Park
3 Comanche Park
4 Century Oaks Park
5 Miner Park
6 Calero Park
7 La Colina Park
8 Albertson Parkway
9 Los Paseos Park

Map 2

Walk 9: Cahalan Park

Location: Cahalan Avenue and Pearlwood Way—easy to find.
                   See Map 2.

Size: 10 acres, about half open grass

Parking: Lot on Pearlwood

For Comfort: Restrooms with wheelchair access, in reasonably
                   clean if somewhat wet condition; water fountain

For Sports: 2 tennis courts, basketball courts, 2 softball fields with
                   bleachers

For Dining: 9 picnic tables, 6 barbecues

For Kids: Playground, bike racks

Description: Moderately rolling, with nice grass. A paved path with
                   lights weaves through about one half of park. Some
                   landscaping. Noticeable but not annoying traffic
                   noise. Unfenced.

Of Note: You can play in the sun on the grass, then retreat to the
                   picnic area for some shade and a seat.

Walk 10: Foothill Park

Location:	Cahalan Avenue off Santa Teresa Blvd.—easy to find. See Map 2.
Size:	6.94 acres, all open natural vegetation
Parking:	Neighborhood street parking
For Comfort:	Water fountain at top
For Kids:	Bike rack at bottom; no bikes allowed in park
Description:	Large hill with twisted live oaks dotted about. Gravel path with steps switchbacks up the hill, saving the climb from being too steep.
Of Note:	This is a real vista point, and the view takes in the whole valley and surrounding hills. Unfortunately, there is plenty of broken glass and other rubbish at the top, so watch where your dog steps.

Walk 11: Comanche Park

Location:	Shawnee Lane off Snell Avenue—easy to find. See Map 2.
Size:	3.01 acres, nearly all open grass
Parking:	Neighborhood street parking
For Comfort:	Water fountain
For Kids:	Playground, bike racks
Description:	Small rolling hills, with grass dying in places, probably from lack of water. Primitive playground. Some shade. Openings in fence along school yard on one side, unfenced into church playing fields on other side.
Of Note:	There is a low-branching tree right at the front of the park, where you can pose your dog quite nicely for photos.

Walk 12: Century Oaks Park

Location: Colleen Drive at Gunter Way, Colleen at Snell Avenue, Colleen at Cottle—hard to find access. See Map 2.

Size: 17.80 acres, all open natural area

Parking: Neighborhood street parking

Description: Undeveloped. A path runs along the flank of the hill, sometimes below high powerlines. Otherwise, it is all open natural vegetation. At Snell, a path starts at the road and leads up the hill. At Cottle you have to climb a low fence to gain access to a natural hillside with a faint path leading up.

Of Note: This may look like a pleasant walk, once you find a way in, but a combination of lots of dog droppings and plenty of eager ticks presents a significant health risk for your dog.

Walk 13: Miner Park

Location: Lean Avenue at Copco Lane—easy to find. See Map 2.

Size: 5.15 acres, nearly all open grass

Parking: Neighborhood street parking

For Comfort: Water fountain

For Sports: Parcourse; softball and soccer fields at adjacent school yard

For Kids: Playground

Description: Slightly rolling, with acceptable grass. Paved path with lights running length of the park. Benches under shade ramada by playground. Busy school yard at back of park.

Of Note: The loop around the parcourse is a nice ramble, but be careful of broken glass in some areas.

Walk 14: Calero Park

Location:	Lean Avenue at Calero Avenue—easy to find. See Map 2.
Size:	4.63 acres, nearly all open grass
Parking:	Neighborhood street parking
For Comfort:	Water fountain
For Dining:	3 picnic tables
For Kids:	Playground
Description:	Slightly rolling, with acceptable grass. Some shade along one side. Backs on active school yard. Lots of dogs can be heard in the back yards facing the park, and there's evidence that many of them visit the park.
Of Note:	Unless you happen to live nearby, there's really not much to bring you to this park.

Walk 15: La Colina Park

Location:	Allegan Circle off Lean Avenue—easy to find. See Map 2.
Size:	25.53 acres, nearly all open grass or natural hillside
Parking:	Neighborhood street parking
For Comfort:	Portable toilets; water fountain
For Sports:	Softball field, soccer field
For Kids:	Playground, bike racks
Description:	Large, flat, open grass area with informal playing fields. Paved path across width, with lights. Dirt path up natural hillside to fine vista point. Community garden adjacent to one side.
Of Note:	This is a big park, with a pleasant grass area and a nice natural area up the hill, with great views from the top.

Walk 16: Albertson Parkway

Location: Purple Hills Drive off Santa Teresa Blvd. See Map 2.

Size: 2.68 acres

Parking: Neighborhood street parking

Description: This is another long, narrow strip under high powerlines that has been made into a pedestrian walkway. A paved path runs from Castillon along Purple Hills for approximately three-fourths mile. Path is almost completely flat. Area on both sides of path resembles a weedy vacant lot, backed by fences of neighbors' houses.

Of Note: If you walk this way for exercise from a house nearby, it's probably convenient. Otherwise, there's little to recommend this park.

Walk 17: Los Paseos Park

Location: Santa Teresa Blvd. near Avenida Espana—easy to find. See Map 2.

Size: 12.17 acres, about three-quarters open grass

Parking: Large lot on Santa Teresa, neighborhood street parking on Via Vista

For Comfort: Restrooms with wheelchair access, in clean condition; water fountains

For Sports: 4 lighted tennis courts, parcourse, softball field

For Dining: 7 picnic tables, 5 barbecues

For Kids: Playground, bike racks

Description: Mostly flat, with some small hills. Grass okay but a bit patchy. Areas of shade, mostly on hill and along section of paved path. Paved path runs across width and most of length of park, with lights. Popular but quiet.

Of Note: Somehow this park seems bigger than it actually is, and it has a little of everything. A snack bar in the building housing the restrooms was closed on my visit.

Walk 18: Santa Teresa County Park

Location: Bernal Road—easy to find. See Map 2.

Size: 1,229 acres; except for the golf course, all open space

Parking: Lot at picnic area

For Comfort: Restrooms with wheelchair access, nice and clean; water fountains; all in picnic area

For Dining: Individual and group picnic areas; group areas must be reserved and paid for; barbecues

Description: Hills in natural grassland condition, with some patches of shade under oaks or conifers. Paths wind around and over hills, most with small gains and losses in elevation. Many trails are also used by equestrians from Buck Norred Stables at boundary of park. Trails are mostly in the sun, varying in distance. Trail maps are at most parking lots.

Of Note: This is a real hiking park, with trails that interconnect and weave through the hills. Deer use the trails as well, so if you're here fairly early or late be alert for them. There are also plenty of ticks.

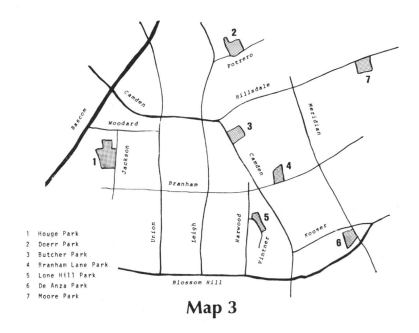

1 Houge Park
2 Doerr Park
3 Butcher Park
4 Branham Lane Park
5 Lone Hill Park
6 De Anza Park
7 Moore Park

Map 3

Walk 19: Houge Park

Location: White Oaks Avenue off Bascom Avenue—maybe a little hard to find. See Map 3.

Size: 11.50 acres, about two-thirds open grass

Parking: Small lot on Stratford, street parking other sides

For Comfort: Fountain

For Sports: 4-station fitness course, soccer field

For Dining: 14 tables, 7 barbecues

For Kids: Large playground

Description: Mostly level, with very nice grass. A long, winding, paved path winds across entire park. A dirt jogging path circles perimeter. Mostly unfenced. Two city buildings on property. Lights along path.

Of Note: This is not a park for a hot sunny day unless you like heat stroke. The only trees are saplings, and even the picnic tables lack shade.

Walk 20: Doerr Park

Location:	Bordered by Park Wilshire Drive, Potrero Drive and Custer Drive, which lie within the square made by Curtner Avenue, Meridian Avenue, Foxworthy Avenue and Leigh Avenue—off main road, but not hard to find. See Map 3.
Size:	11.69 acres, about half open grass
Parking:	Neighborhood street parking
For Comfort:	Restrooms with wheelchair access, in reasonably clean condition; water fountain
For Sports:	4 tennis courts, basketball courts, softball field
For Kids:	Playground
Description:	Knoll at one corner, otherwise flat. Lush grass with few, if any, burrs. Unfenced. Paved path across width and half of length of park. Nice shady area around picnic tables. Quiet neighborhood.
Of Note:	There are lots of park benches scattered around, for those who like to sit and watch the world go by.

Walk 21: Butcher Park

Location:	Camden Avenue between Lancaster Drive and Oakwood Avenue—on main road, easy to find. See Map 3.
Size:	10 acres, about half open grass
Parking:	Neighborhood street parking
For Comfort:	Restrooms with wheelchair access, in reasonably clean condition; water fountain
For Sports:	Lighted basketball courts, soccer field, softball field with bleachers
For Dining:	12 picnic tables, 8 barbecues
For Kids:	Playground

Description: Flat area, mostly grass. Fenced only on the Camden side. Short paved path around the basketball courts. Plenty of large shade trees. Noticeable traffic noise from Camden.

Of Note: One tree has grown at such an angle that dogs can easily run up the trunk and view the world from new heights. This not only offers fun for your dog, but provides a unique photo opportunity.

Walk 22: Branham Lane Park

Location: Branham Lane between Camden Avenue and Kirk Road—on main road, easy to find. See Map 3.

Size: 5.75 acres, nearly all open grass

Parking: Small lot for approximately 12 cars

For Comfort: Water fountain

For Dining: 2 picnic tables

Description: Fairly level, lawnlike grass with hardly any burrs. Fenced only on side facing shopping center, not on Branham. Limited shade. Noticeable traffic noise from Branham. Two nearly flat paved paths, with lights.

Of Note: There is broken glass all along the parking lot area, so don't let your dog wander there. One side of the park currently faces an abandoned orchard, but there's no telling what development may bring.

Walk 23: Lone Hill Park

Location: Michon Drive off Camden Avenue—could be hard to find if you don't know the area. See Map 3.

Size: 7.87 acres, about two-thirds open grass

Parking: Neighborhood street parking

For Comfort: Restrooms with wheelchair access, in reasonably clean condition; water fountain

For Sports: Basketball courts, volleyball court

For Dining: 16 picnic tables, 3 barbecues

For Kids: 2 playground areas

Description: Hill along one side, sloping down to level area. Grass a little sparse, but not too weedy. Fenced along neighbors' back yards. Paved path around picnic and play areas. Limited shade. Fairly quiet location.

Of Note: One playground section has equipment that dogs can enjoy, too, with wooden platforms at different heights. There are also large rocks to climb on.

Walk 24: De Anza Park
(formerly Arroyo Park)

Location: Meridian Avenue between Princeton Drive and Helmond Lane—on main road, easy to find. See Map 3.

Size: 9.61 acres, less than half open grass

Parking: Neighborhood street parking

For Comfort: Restrooms, somewhat less than clean; water fountain

For Sports: Softball field with bleachers, basketball courts, paddle tennis courts

For Dining: 6 picnic tables, 3 barbecues

For Kids: Playground

Description: Flat area, mostly grass. Completely unfenced. Some shade. Lights in the playground and basketball areas. Lots of traffic and residential noise.

Of Note: There was an unpleasant amount of rubbish and broken glass scattered all over the park. Dogs' paws could suffer here.

Walk 25: Paul Moore Park

Location: Cherry Avenue off Hillsdale Avenue. See Map 3.

Size: 8.40 acres, about three-quarters open grass

Parking: Neighborhood street parking

For Comfort: Restrooms with wheelchair access, in pretty clean condition; water fountain

For Sports: 4 lighted tennis courts, basketball courts, soccer field, softball field with bleachers

For Dining: 6 picnic tables, 3 barbecues

For Kids: Playground, bike racks

Description: Hilly on one side of the park, flat in the rest. Nice grass. Rough paved path over the hill and across length of park. Fenced on Hillsdale side. Less traffic noise than you would expect from Hillsdale.

Of Note: The playground equipment is very unusual, including a valley and hills made of tires, to be climbed to reach high platforms.

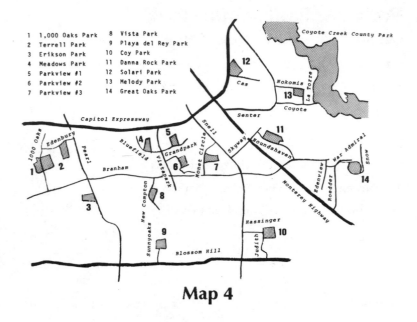

1	1,000 Oaks Park	8	Vista Park
2	Terrell Park	9	Playa del Rey Park
3	Erikson Park	10	Coy Park
4	Meadows Park	11	Danna Rock Park
5	Parkview #1	12	Solari Park
6	Parkview #2	13	Melody Park
7	Parkview #3	14	Great Oaks Park

Map 4

Walk 26: Thousand Oaks Park

Location: Normington Way or 1000 Oaks Drive in area of Branham Lane and Capitol Expwy.—relatively easy to find. See Map 4.

Size: 10.01 acres, nearly all open space

Parking: Neighborhood street parking

For Comfort: Water fountain

For Dining: 2 picnic tables

For Kids: Playground

Description: The name is a bit of an exaggeration, but this is an oak grove, with redwood chips laid down under the oaks and dirt trails weaving everywhere. Sunny, grassy areas occupy two corners of the park. Flat, with lots of shade. Benches are scattered around. Very quiet.

Of Note: This is a gorgeous, seminatural area, with many squirrels providing the entertainment. Well worth a visit.

Walk 27: Terrell Park

Location:	Kenton Lane and Normington Way, near Branham Lane and Capitol Expwy.—not bad to find. See Map 4.
Size:	5.40 acres, about three-quarters open grass
Parking:	Neighborhood street parking
For Comfort:	Water fountain
For Dining:	3 picnic tables
For Kids:	Playground, bike racks
Description:	Rolling terrain with very nice grass. Pleasant areas of shade in several places. Paved paths running in loops through park, with lights. Next to busy school, so lots of kid noise during recess. Otherwise quiet neighborhood.
Of Note:	This is a nice-sized open area, and the looping paths make a good ramble; then you can rest in the shade.

Walk 28: Leif Erikson Park
(also known as Oyster Bay)

Location:	Pearl Avenue on the front side, Fell Avenue on the back—hard to find your way around to the back where the parking is. See Map 4.
Size:	1 acre, mostly open grass
Parking:	Neighborhood street parking on Fell and Oyster Bay Drive
For Comfort:	Water fountain
For Dining:	4 picnic tables, 3 barbecues
For Kids:	Playground
Description:	Moderately hilly, with nice grass and small shade trees. Paved paths loop through the length of the park, making it seem bigger than it is. Lights along paths. Traffic noise from Pearl in half of park nearer that road.

Of Note: This is a nice small neighborhood park, but getting around to the back side where you can park is a challenge, particularly if your map shows roads which don't exist, as mine does.

Walk 29: Meadows Park

Location: Bluefield Drive off Capitol Expressway—easy to find. See Map 4.

Size: 4 acres, mostly open grass

Parking: Neighborhood street parking

For Comfort: Water fountain

For Dining: 5 picnic tables, 2 barbecues

For Kids: Playground

Description: Slightly rolling terrain, nice grass. Some shade, mostly around picnic areas. Paved path across front of park. Nice quiet neighborhood.

Of Note: This is one of several small neighborhood parks in the area, convenient to the people who live here, but not really worth a visit from the rest of us.

Walk 30: Parkview #1

Location: Bluefield Drive off Capitol Expressway—easy to find. See Map 4.

Size: 2.63 acres, mostly open grass

Parking: Neighborhood street parking

For Comfort: Water fountain

For Kids: Playground

Description: Slightly rolling terrain, nice lush grass. Good shade areas. Some benches near the playground. Paved paths across park, with lights. Quiet neighborhood.

Of Note: There are three Parkview parks; this is the most attractive, with extremely well done landscaping. It's small, but a pleasant place.

Walk 31: Parkview #2

Location:	Grandpark Circle off Vistapark Drive—a little harder to find. See Map 4.
Size:	2.58 acres, mostly open space
Parking:	Neighborhood street parking
For Comfort:	Water fountain
For Kids:	Playground, bike racks
Description:	Rolling small hills with grass, except for the large playground at one end. Some shade. Paved path down length of park. Quiet neighborhood.
Of Note:	This is the middle one of the three Parkview parks, and that is where it falls in appeal. Not as attractive as Parkview #1, but a step up from Parkview #3. Unless you live nearby, don't bother to find this one.

Walk 32: Parkview #3

Location:	Sayoko Circle off Snell Avenue—easy to find. See Map 4.
Size:	5.44 acres, almost all open grass
Parking:	Neighborhood street parking
For Comfort:	Water fountain
Description:	Flat, with nice grass. Two paved paths run across park, with lights. No shade, no landscaping. Dogs running loose during my visit.
Of Note:	This is the largest and the least attractive of the three Parkview parks. It's really just an empty lot with grass—a good place for a run if you live nearby, and lots of dogs do.

Walk 33: Vista Park

Location:	New Compton Drive off Hyde Park Drive. See Map 4.
Size:	1.43 acres, nearly all open grass

Parking: Neighborhood street parking, and a lot on Hyde Park

For Sports: Softball and soccer fields

Description: The acreage given by San Jose Parks and Recreation does not agree with what you find when you visit—the park is actually much bigger. However, it's flat and offers hardly any shade, and is not overly attractive.

Of Note: This is a large open area to meander around, but there's not much of interest.

Walk 34: Playa Del Ray Park

Location: Sunny Oaks Drive off Blossom Hill Road—easy to find. See Map 4.

Size: 3.67 acres, about half open grass

Parking: Neighborhood street parking

For Comfort: Water fountain

For Sports: Basketball courts

For Dining: 5 picnic tables, 1 barbecue

For Kids: Playground, bike racks

Description: Mostly level, with lush grass. Paved path with lights runs diagonally across park. Nice areas of shade, plus shade arbor over benches at playground area.

Of Note: A pleasant-looking park, though small. The playground includes a concrete tunnel, useful if you're working on agility.

Walk 35: Coy Park

Location: Sigrid Way off Chynoweth Avenue. See Map 4.

Size: 9.65 acres

Parking: Neighborhood street parking

Description: A large empty lot of rubble and weeds tucked in amid several new housing developments.

Of Note: At the time of my visit, this looked like an unplowed field, but with all the new housing in the area, it may be under development soon. If you're interested in future plans for this park, contact the San Jose Parks and Recreation Department.

Walk 36: Danna Rock Outcropping

Location: Houndshaven Way off Skyway Drive—pretty easy to find. See Map 4.

Size: 10.98 acres, all open space other than a small playground

Parking: Neighborhood street parking

For Comfort: Water fountain, but not functioning on my visit

For Sports: Small fitness area

For Dining: 3 picnic tables, 2 barbecues

For Kids: Playground

Description: Flat grassy area is backed by an impressive hill studded with rocks. Paved path runs across the front and loops through the park. No shade, and—at least when I visited—no water. Nice quiet neighborhood with lots of dogs in the houses nearby.

Of Note: This park offers a nice climb, with a good view at the top. Unfortunately, the entire rock area at the top is littered with broken glass. Rocks seem to make an irresistible target for bottles. This is a park with a difference, and would be a great place if it weren't for the glass.

Walk 37: Louis S. Solari Park/Center

Location:	Cas Drive off Ezie Street off Senter Road. See Map 4.
Size:	9.47 acres, only about one-quarter open grass
Parking:	Neighborhood street parking
For Comfort:	Restrooms with wheelchair access, reasonably clean; water fountain
For Sports:	Tetherball, 3 lighted tennis courts, basketball courts, lighted softball field with bleachers, lighted soccer field
For Dining:	7 picnic tables, 6 barbecues
For Kids:	Playground, bike racks
Description:	Flat, with most of the open grass being on the softball and soccer fields. Nice shady areas. Community center buildings are still going up. Lots of traffic noise from Capitol Expressway.
Of Note:	There are all sorts of sports facilities if you like to play and your dog likes to lie and watch.

Walk 38: Melody Park

Location:	Nokomis Drive off Senter Road—easy to find. See Map 4.
Size:	4.02 acres, mostly open grass
Parking:	Neighborhood street parking
For Comfort:	Water fountain was not functional on my visit
For Dining:	8 picnic tables, 4 barbecues
For Kids:	Playground, bike racks
Description:	Slightly hilly, with sparse grass. One of the most primitive playgrounds I've seen in a San Jose park. Water fountain vandalized and graffiti on the signs and slide. Nice shade areas.
Of Note:	Park was empty during my visit, but from the signs of vandalism, this could be a rowdy and maybe even unpleasant place on weekends or evenings.

Walk 39: Great Oaks Park

Location: Giusti Drive and Snow Drive—a little hard to find, and if you're approaching from the Hellyer Avenue side, some fierce, hilly streets to climb. See Map 4.

Size: 12.26 acres, nearly all open grass

Parking: Neighborhood street parking

For Comfort: Water fountain

For Sports: Basketball courts, softball field with bleachers

For Kids: Playground, under construction during my visit

Description: Slightly rolling terrain, lovely grass. The beautiful oak trees for which the park is named provide shade. Paved paths across both sides of park. Quiet except for dogs in back yards facing the park, who know when you go by with your dog.

Of Note: There is a truly massive oak in the middle of one of the paths, with benches situated around it. This is a beautiful park, and a great place to sit and relax.

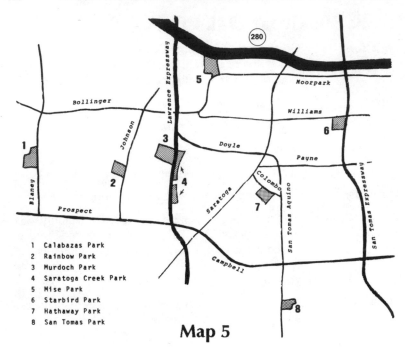

1   Calabazas Park
2   Rainbow Park
3   Murdoch Park
4   Saratoga Creek Park
5   Mise Park
6   Starbird Park
7   Hathaway Park
8   San Tomas Park

Map 5

Walk 40: Calabazas Park

Location: Blaney Avenue between Rainbow Drive and Chiala Lane—on main road, easy to find. See Map 5.

Size: 17.09 acres, about three-quarters open grass or dirt

Parking: Sizable lot off Blaney; also street parking on Blaney and Rainbow

For Comfort: Restrooms with wheelchair access, in good condition; water fountain

For Sports: 3 tennis courts, horseshoe pits, basketball courts, lighted softball field with bleachers

For Dining: 6 tables

For Kids: Playground, bike racks

Description: Some small hills on the Blaney side, then mostly flat until you reach the gully where Calabazas Creek sometimes flows. The grass has been sacrificed to the drought. Paved area around the restroom and play area. Lots of shade along the gully. The ground is somewhat uneven in the section toward the gully.

Of Note: Whether the creek is wet or dry, the gully is a fascinating place to walk a dog. Birds and ground squirrels are everywhere.

Walk 41: Rainbow Park

Location: Johnson Avenue between Donington Drive and Rainbow Drive. See Map 5.

Size: 9.61 acres

Parking: Neighborhood street parking

Description: Slightly rolling, but otherwise hard to tell, as the park was under construction during my visit. It looks as though a major makeover is just beginning. The park is closed during construction, but the Rainbow Community Center is still open.

Walk 42: Murdoch Park

Location: Wunderlich Drive and Castle Glen Avenue; one side runs along Lawrence Expressway between Bollinger Road and Prospect Road, but you can't get in from Lawrence—could be hard to find. See Map 5.

Size: 11.50 acres, about half open grass

Parking: Neighborhood street parking

For Comfort: Restrooms, in reasonably clean condition; water fountain

For Sports: 4 tennis courts; school next door has softball/soccer field and basketball courts

For Dining: Giant barbecue pit, 2 barbecues, 8 picnic tables

For Kids: 2 playgrounds

Description: Slightly rolling, mostly grass. Fenced along school yard except for athletic fields. Long paved path wind-

ing through park, with lights. Plenty of shade. Lots of
benches scattered around. Fairly quiet.

Of Note: If you're interested in agility courses for your dog, the
playgrounds offer a chance for some practice. They
have a tunnel, horizontal beams at various heights,
and wooden platforms on springs.

Walk 43: South and North Saratoga Creek Park

Location: Along Lawrence Expressway, but reachable only by
minor streets named Graves, Lassen, Eileen, Hoyet,
and Forest Court, between Prospect Road and Doyle
Road—hard to find if you don't know the area. See
Map 5.

Size: South is 2.82 acres, North is 7.64 acres, all open grass
or dirt

Parking: Small lots on Hoyet and Eileen; street parking on
Graves, Lassen, and Forest Court

For Comfort: Restrooms in North section; water fountains at both
ends of North section, fountain in South section not
functioning on my visit

For Sports: Parcourse running through both sections

For Dining: 8 picnic tables scattered along path in North section, 4
barbecues

For Kids: Playground in North section, bike racks

Description: Slightly rolling, all grass in North section, half grass
and half dirt in South section. Paved path running
completely through both sections, with lights.
Benches here and there. Some shade.

Of Note: The perfect park for dog owners in wheelchairs. The
path is wide and smoothly paved, running from sun to
shade and back again for nearly a half mile.

Walk 44: Mise Park

Location:	Moorpark Avenue between John Mise Court and Park Meadow Drive—on main road, easy to find. See Map 5.
Size:	11.71 acres, about three-quarters open grass
Parking:	Lot for about 40 cars on John Mise Court, but this is also used by apartment dwellers across the court; neighborhood street parking on Park Meadow
For Comfort:	Restrooms with wheelchair access, in rather dumpy condition; water fountain
For Sports:	Softball field with bleachers and lights, basketball courts
For Dining:	6 picnic tables
For Kids:	Playground, bike racks
Description:	Rolling hills at one end, otherwise fairly flat. Nice grass with few weeds. A couple of shade areas. Unfenced except where it backs on Highway 280. Paved around restrooms and playground. Lights throughout park. Considerable traffic noise from 280.
Of Note:	One of the items in the playground is a mockup of a pioneer wagon, providing another photo opportunity.

Walk 45: Starbird Park

Location:	San Tomas Expressway and Williams Road—on main roads, easy to find. See Map 5.
Size:	8.23 acres, about one-third open grass
Parking:	Parking lot at Community Center, and neighborhood street parking
For Comfort:	Restrooms with wheelchair access, sparkling clean; water fountain
For Sports:	Horseshoe pits, basketball courts, softball field
For Dining:	14 picnic tables, 4 barbecues
For Kids:	Playground

Description: Flat area with some landscaping, including flowers. Fenced on San Tomas side. Paved path around playground and Community Center. Shade trees around picnic area. Noticeable traffic noise from San Tomas.

Of Note: The Community Center makes this a busy and well-lit place. The landscaping is attractive, but the actual room for walking is limited.

Walk 46: Hathaway Park

Location: Colombo Drive between Saratoga Avenue and San Tomas Aquino Road—streets in this area can be a little confusing. See Map 5.

Size: 7.69 acres, mostly open grass

Parking: Neighborhood street parking

For Comfort: Restrooms with wheelchair access, in reasonably clean condition; water fountain

For Sports: Jogging path with parcourse, basketball courts, softball field with bleachers

For Dining: 10 picnic tables scattered around, 5 barbecues

For Kids: Playground, bike racks

Description: Slightly rolling, mostly grass. Fenced along neighbors' back yards. Paved path around perimeter. Some shade. Quiet neighborhood.

Of Note: The jogging path around the perimeter makes a pleasant ramble, and is especially accessible to those in wheelchairs. Dogs can even try some of the parcourse equipment.

Walk 47: San Tomas Park

Location: San Tomas Aquino Road and Valerie Drive—not hard to find. See Map 5.

Size: 4.76 acres, about half open grass

Parking: No parking is allowed along the Valerie side of the
                   park, but street parking is available on San Tomas
                   Aquino

For Comfort: Restrooms with wheelchair access, in clean condi-
                   tion; water fountain

For Sports: Basketball courts

For Dining: 14 tables, 6 barbecues

For Kids: Playground, bike racks

Description: Hilly around the street perimeters, but flat otherwise.
                   Good lush grass. Fenced only along neighbors' back
                   yards. Paved path cutting across most of park from
                   Valerie to San Tomas Aquino, and taking in play area
                   and restrooms. Lots of shade. Quiet neighborhood.

Of Note: Some planted areas and large shade trees of various
                   sorts make the park visually appealing.

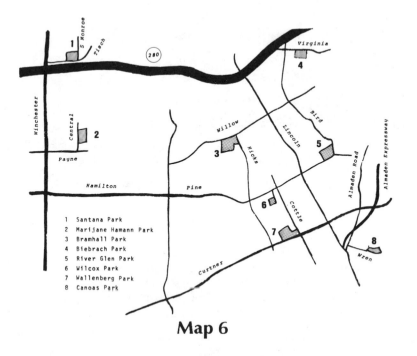

1 Santana Park
2 Marijane Hamann Park
3 Bramhall Park
4 Biebrach Park
5 River Glen Park
6 Wilcox Park
7 Wallenberg Park
8 Canoas Park

Map 6

Walk 48: Santana Park

Location: Tisch Way off Winchester Blvd.. See Map 6.

Size: 5.32 acres, nearly all open space

Parking: Lot on Baywood

For Comfort: Restrooms with wheelchair access, somewhat dirty; water fountain

For Sports: Softball field

For Dining: 3 picnic tables

Description: Flat, with scrubby grass. Fenced except on side where pedestrian walkway leads over Highway 280. Traffic noise from 280. Some shade around edges.

Of Note: The traffic noise from 280 is at an unpleasant, almost unbearable level.

Walk 49: Marijane Hamann Park

Location: Central Avenue off Payne Road—hard to find. See Map 6.

Size: 10.51 acres, mostly open grass

Parking: Neighborhood street parking

For Comfort: Restrooms in Korean American Community Services building, very clean; water fountain

For Sports: 3 tennis courts, softball field with bleachers, soccer field

For Dining: 8 picnic tables, 4 barbecues

For Kids: Playground, bike racks

Description: A few tiny hills, otherwise flat. Grass a little sparse. No paved path. Lights around building. Lots of big shade trees. Next to pedestrian overcrossing of Highway 17. Lots of traffic noise from 17.

Of Note: In autumn, you can actually see some leaves changing colors in this park and along Central Avenue.

Walk 50: Frank Bramhall Park

Location: Willow Street off Meridian Aveneue—easy to find. See Map 6.

Size: 15.39 acres, about two-thirds open grass

Parking: Lots along Camino Ramon and Britton streets, street parking on Willow

For Comfort: Restrooms with wheelchair access, reasonably clean; water fountain

For Sports: Lawn bowling, shuffleboard, 6 tennis courts, basketball courts, volleyball court, softball field with bleachers

For Dining: 30 tables, 6 barbecues

For Kids: Playground, bike racks

Description: Flat except for depressed area at one edge. Lovely tree-lined paths across width and length of park. Lights in some areas. Unfenced. Lots of shade trees and plenty of squirrels.

Of Note: Most of the trees are either oaks or redwoods, including some redwoods of decent size, making the park very attractive. If you're curious, you have a chance to watch some lawn bowling.

Walk 51: Biebrach Park

Location: Virginia Street off Bird Avenue—relatively easy to find. See Map 6.

Size: 6.02 acres, about two-thirds open grass

Parking: Neighborhood street parking

For Comfort: Restrooms, with no doors on stalls and lots of graffiti; water fountain

For Sports: Swimming pool, basketball courts, soccer field, softball field

For Dining: 6 picnic tables, 1 barbecue

For Kids: Playground, bike racks

Description: Flat, grass somewhat sparse. Paved path only around restrooms and community center. Fenced along front and back and around pool. Limited shade. Not a good neighborhood.

Of Note: A woman alone could feel a bit uncomfortable here, even with a dog.

Walk 52: River Glen Park

Location: Bird Avenue and Pine Avenue. See Map 6.

Size: 8.97 acres, mostly open grass

Parking: Neighborhood street parking

For Comfort: Restrooms with wheelchair access, in pretty good condition; water fountains

For Sports: Shuffleboard, 2 tennis courts, volleyball court, basketball courts, softball fields

For Dining: 7 picnic tables, 5 barbecues

For Kids: Playground, bike racks

Description: Flat, with grass dying from lack of water due to the drought. Little shade to be found. Fenced completely around.

Of Note: If San Jose ever follows Mountain View in allowing off-leash work for obedience training, this could be a good place to start because of the fencing all the way around the park. Joggers use an informal path outside the fence around the perimeter.

Walk 53: Wilcox Park

Location: Wilcox Way off Pine Avenue. See Map 6.

Size: 1.97 acres, all open grass

Parking: Neighborhood street parking

Description: Flat, with nice grass. Good patches of shade. Fenced along neighbors' back yards.

Of Note: This is really just a patch of grass, equivalent to a large country-style lot, but if it happens to be near your house, it's a pleasant place to go.

Walk 54: Raoul Wallenberg Park

Location: Curtner Avenue between Cottle and Cherry avenues. See Map 6.

Size: 9.50 acres, about two-thirds open grass

Parking: On Cherry or on Madrona; to get to the park you can either walk out to and along Curtner or squeeze through the opening in the fence around some playing fields and walk toward the tennis courts at the back of the park

For Comfort: Restrooms with wheelchair access, in exceptionally clean condition; water fountains

For Sports: Parcourse, 4 tennis courts

For Dining: Picnic tables, barbecues

For Kids: Playground

Description: Slightly rolling terrain, with very nice grass. Little shade is available. Good paved path nearly completely around the park, with lights. Surprisingly little traffic noise from Curtner.

Of Note: A plaque here explains the park's dedication to Raoul Wallenberg, and it just feels good being in this park.

Walk 55: Canoas Park

Location: End of Wren Drive near Almaden Expwy.—nearly impossible to find. See Map 6.

Size: 2.10 acres, about half open grass

Parking: Neighborhood street parking

For Comfort: Water fountain

For Sports: 2 tennis courts

For Dining: 6 picnic tables, 2 barbecues

For Kids: Playground, bike racks

Description: Flat, with sparse grass. Some shade available. Paved path across park from Wren to Thrush Drive. Lights.

Of Note: Unless you live in the area, don't try to find this one. Working your way through the maze of little streets isn't worth it.

Walk 56: Coyote Creek County Park

Location: Along Senter Road to Hellyer Avenue, then along Highway 101—easy to see, but difficult to find access. See Map 7.

Size: 385.55 acres, all open natural land

Parking: Street parking

Description: Can gain access to section between Capitol Expressway and Tully Road at the back of Senter Park—trail running along creek connects with trail through county park—about 1½ miles from one road to the other.

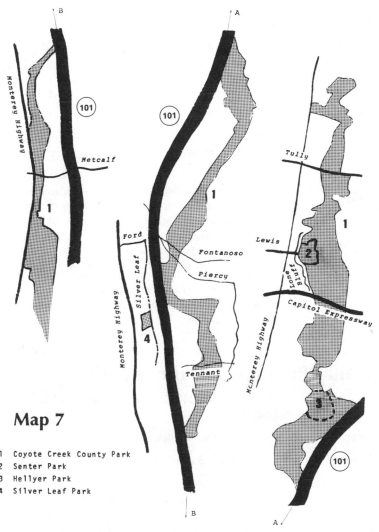

Map 7

1 Coyote Creek County Park
2 Senter Park
3 Hellyer Park
4 Silver Leaf Park

Can gain access to section between Capitol Expressway and 101 at end of Palisades off Hellyer—dirt trail runs for about 2 miles.

Of Note: This is completely undeveloped territory, with dirt tracks mostly worn down by walkers. Some of the climbs out of the gully are steep. The creek is dry much of the distance for much of the year. Lots of ticks and fleas lie in wait.

Walk 57: Senter Park

Location: Lone Bluff Way off Senter Road. See Map 7.

Size: 8 acres, mostly in a natural state

Parking: Limited street parking; small dirt area at gate of park

For Comfort: Restrooms still exist but do not look functional

For Sports: Home of the San Jose Golden Eagles Horseshoe Club; horseshoe pits are behind a fence and not open to the public

Description: Paved path in a loop around the park, also a dirt path along the creek. Some broken glass on the first section of the paved path. Other than fenced horseshoe area, entire park is in natural state. A dog lives behind the fence in the horseshoe area, and barks as you pass.

Of Note: This is a good place to pick up the dirt trail along the creek, which continues into the Coyote Creek County Park Chain. You can walk to Capitol Expressway in one direction and Tully Road in the other.

Walk 58: Hellyer County Park

Location: Palisade Drive off Hellyer Avenue—hard to find. See Map 7.

Size: 223 acres, mostly open space

Parking: Neighborhood street parking

Description: While the official County materials specify that dogs are allowed in the "Claitor" area of the park, a large NO DOGS ALLOWED sign greets you at the entrance to the park. With so many other parks in the area, why fight it? Avoid this one and go somewhere else.

Walk 59: Silver Leaf Park

Location:	Palmwell off Monterey Highway—easy to find. See Map 7.
Size:	5.80 acres, nearly all open grass
Parking:	Neighborhood street parking
For Comfort:	Water fountain, not functional on my visit
For Sports:	4-station parcourse
For Dining:	7 picnic tables
For Kids:	Playground, bike racks
Description:	Slightly rolling, with a nice open grass area. Paved path with lights across one end only. Very little shade. Quiet.
Of Note:	If you like to romp and lie in the grass in the sun, this could be the park for you.

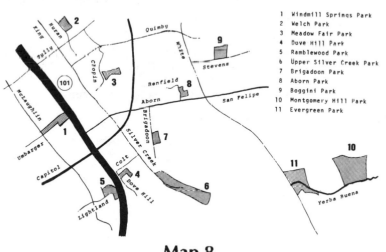

1   Windmill Springs Park
2   Welch Park
3   Meadow Fair Park
4   Dove Hill Park
5   Ramblewood Park
6   Upper Silver Creek Park
7   Brigadoon Park
8   Aborn Park
9   Boggini Park
10   Montgomery Hill Park
11   Evergreen Park

Map 8

Walk 60: Windmill Springs

Location:	End of Umbarger Road off McLaughlin Avenue—fairly easy to find. (Note that Umbarger does not go through from Monterey Highway to the park.) See Map 8.
Size:	8.31 acres, mostly open grass
Parking:	Neighborhood street parking
For Comfort:	Water fountain
For Sports:	5 chess tables, fitness station
For Dining:	6 picnic tables
For Kids:	Playground
Description:	Slightly rolling terrain, sparse grass. Little shade. A paved path runs through the park and part way down a narrow strip of green running under the high-tension powerlines. Path is lighted.
Of Note:	If you just want a short, paved ramble and a game of chess, this is the place for you. The chess tables are in the shade around the playground.

Walk 61: Robert Welch Park

Location:	Huran Drive off Tully Road—easy to find. See Map 8.
Size:	11.09 acres, mostly open grass
Parking:	Neighborhood street parking, but not on the park side of any bordering streets on weekends or holidays
For Comfort:	Restrooms, with wheelchair access, reasonably clean; water fountain
For Sports:	2 softball fields with bleachers
For Dining:	5 tables, 5 barbecues
For Kids:	Playground, bike racks
Description:	Mostly flat, with some small hills. Grass nothing special. A small amount of shade. Paved path only to the restrooms.

Of Note: A large egret was walking sedately across the park throughout our visit, and did not seem impressed by our presence. If for some reason you have been visiting the many undeveloped parks in the area, this is a good place to find a restroom.

Walk 62: Meadow Fair Park

Location: Sibelius Avenue and Chopin Avenue off Quimby Road—nearly impossible to find. See Map 8.

Size: 8.41 acres

Description: This is another of San Jose's "undeveloped" parks, meaning that right now there is nothing here worth a visit. There is an open area of rubble field behind a row of somewhat run-down houses, with no apparent way of even getting to the field. Currently, this is certainly not worth taking the trouble to find. If you are interested in future plans for this area, contact the San Jose Parks and Recreation Department.

Walk 63: Dove Hill Park

Location: Ravens Place Way off Silver Creek Road—nearly impossible to find. See Map 8.

Size: 3.91 acres

Description: When San Jose calls a park "undeveloped," it doesn't mean that there aren't any restrooms—it means that the park does not yet exist. There's some open land in the area that might be a future park, but right now there's nothing worth winding through little housing-development streets for. A new development is just going in, so the park may come into being some time soon. Check with San Jose Parks and Recreation if you're interested in the plans for this area.

Walk 64: Ramblewood Park

Location: Dundale Drive off Alvernaz Drive off McLaughlin Avenue. See Map 8.

Size: 9.34 acres, almost all open space, some grass and some dirt and rocks

Parking: Neighborhood street parking

For Comfort: Restrooms with wheelchair access, reasonably clean; water fountain

For Dining: 12 picnic tables, 4 barbecues

For Kids: Playground

Description: Large hill at one side, with dirt and rocks. Nice grass on flat area. Not much shade. Paved path up and down hill and across park to far edge, with lights. At top of hill, good view of surrounding hills but lots of traffic noise from 101.

Of Note: There is lots of broken glass in the hill section, cleaned up every week, but back again almost immediately. The rocks seem to be irresistible targets for bottles.

Walk 65: Upper Silver Creek Park

Location: End of Silver Creek Road—easy to find. See Map 8.

Size: 37.19 acres

Description: While the end of Silver Creek Road may be easy to find, it may be hard to believe that you're at the edge of a park when you get there. This is another "undeveloped" park. You can walk in on the road, for it extends past where you can drive, but you soon encounter fences for cattle pasture. This will be a large, hilly park when it is developed, but for the present it offers little reason for a visit. If you are interested in future plans for this park, contact the San Jose Parks and Recreation Department.

Walk 66: Brigadoon Park

Location: Brigadoon Way off Aborn Road—easy to find. See Map 8.

Size: 5.49 acres

Parking: Limited neighborhood street parking

For Comfort: Water fountain

For Sports: Sand volleyball court

For Dining: 12 tables, 6 barbecues

For Kids: Playground, cement slides, bike racks

Description: There's one big hill with two very steep cement slides winding down it; otherwise mostly flat. Not much shade. A good paved path runs all the way around and through the park, with lights.

Of Note: If you really want to try something different, take a turn at the cement slides.

Walk 67: Aborn Park

Location: Renfield Way off Aborn Road—easy to find, but somewhat hard to recognize as a park. See Map 8.

Size: 2.31 acres, all open grass and rubble

Parking: Neighborhood street parking on Renfield

Description: Really just a dirt and grass lot with a dirt path to Aborn Road. The creekbed is littered with garbage and the path and surrounding area are strewn with broken glass.

Of Note: This is not a very attractive place, but my dog seemed to find the smells and sounds quite interesting.

Walk 68: Boggini Park

Location: Stevens Lane off White Road—easy to find. See Map 8.

Size:	9.97 acres, over three-quarters open grass
Parking:	Neighborhood street parking
For Comfort:	Water fountain
For Sports:	Playing fields at adjacent school
For Dining:	20 picnic tables, 7 barbecues
For Kids:	Playground, bike racks
Description:	Hilly terrain, nice grass. Good number of mid-size fir trees for shade. Paved path just around playground.
Of Note:	On my visit there were cats all over the place, presumably from the houses across Millbrook. Keep a firm hold on your dog here!

Walk 69: Montgomery Hill Park

Location:	Yerba Buena Road off San Felipe Road—nearly impossible to find. See Map 8.
Size:	59.60 acres
Description:	Although the map shows a large green park, at the present time there is Evergreen Valley College, then fenced cattle range, then a granite quarry, and finally another fenced cattle ranch. There is one small unfenced area with a sign for Evergreen Park, but this is only a tiny patch of weedy property on one side of the road and an open field on the other. Montgomery Hill is listed in San Jose parks literature as having a "historical vista," but it looks as if we will all have to wait until the park is developed to see it. If you are interested in future plans for this park, contact the San Jose Parks and Recreation Department.

Walk 70: Evergreen Park

Location:	Yerba Buena Road—easy to find, hard to understand. See Map 8.
Size:	27.46 acres, nearly all open space

Parking:	Street parking
For Comfort:	Restrooms; water fountain?
For Dining:	22 picnic tables, 5 barbecues?
Description:	At one side of the road is Yerba Buena Creek, trees and natural vegetation lining its banks. At the other side of the road is a large open meadow.
Of Note:	I must admit that I saw the sign indicating I was indeed at Evergreen Park, but I did not see any picnic tables or restrooms or anything other than what's in the above description. What I presumed was part of the college may actually be the facilities for this park.

Walk 71: Columbus Park

Location:	West Coleman Street and Walnut Street—easy to find. See Map 9.
Size:	9.91 acres, about three-quarters open grass
Parking:	Neighborhood street parking
For Comfort:	Restrooms with wheelchair access, reasonably clean; water fountain
For Sports:	Volleyball courts, basketball courts, lighted softball field with bleachers
For Dining:	8 picnic tables, 3 barbecues
For Kids:	Primitive playground
Description:	Flat, with sparse grass and a severe mole problem. Paved only around the restrooms. Fenced on three sides. A triple threat of noise—from cars, planes and trains.
Of Note:	This park seems to be directly under San Jose Airport's landing path, and the jets are very low as they pass overhead.

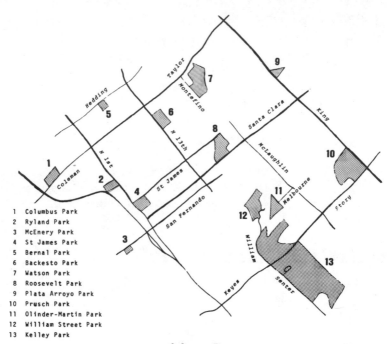

1 Columbus Park
2 Ryland Park
3 McEnery Park
4 St James Park
5 Bernal Park
6 Backesto Park
7 Watson Park
8 Roosevelt Park
9 Plata Arroyo Park
10 Prusch Park
11 Olinder-Martin Park
12 William Street Park
13 Kelley Park

Map 9

Walk 72: Ryland Park

Location: San Pedro Street and Fox Avenue—hard to find. See Map 9.

Size: 3.15 acres, about one-third open grass

Parking: Lot on San Pedro

For Comfort: Restrooms, with wheelchair access, clean; water fountains

For Sports: Swimming pool, basketball courts, parcourse, 3 chess tables

For Dining: 10 picnic tables, 3 barbecues

For Kids: Playground, bike racks

Description: Flat, with good grass. A lovely, huge shade tree in the middle, with chess tables around it. Fenced on three sides. Quiet except for an occasional plane overhead. Palm plaza with benches on the First Street side.

Of Note: This is an extremely pleasant little park, with decorative lamps along its path, fancy water fountains, and a mural on the freeway overpass. But it can be hard to get to.

Walk 73: John P. McEnery Park

Location: San Fernando Street off Almaden Blvd.—easy to find. See Map 9.

Size: 1.83 acres, about one-third open grass

Parking: A definite problem, with only pay lots for several blocks

For Comfort: Restrooms, with wheelchair access, clean

For Sports: 4 lighted tennis courts

Description: A small, mostly flat park, half taken up by tennis courts. There is also a plaza with some statuary in the center.

Of Note: Parking is too much of a problem to make an effort to visit this small park.

Walk 74: St. James Park and Senior Center

Location: East St. James Street at North 1st Street—easy to find if you know which way the one-way streets run. See Map 9.

Size: 7.01 acres, with little open space

Parking: Street parking with parking meters

For Comfort: Restrooms open only for special events; water fountain

For Sports: Fitness cluster

For Dining: 1 picnic table

Description: Flat, heavily landscaped area, with senior center at front.

Of Note: This park is located amid a maze of one-way streets, and all parking in the area is on parking meters.

Walk 75: Bernal Park

Location: North 7th Street at Hedding Street—easy to find. See Map 9.

Size: 2.25 acres, nearly all open grass

Parking: Small lot on 7th

For Comfort: Restrooms, with wheelchair access, not too clean

For Sports: Softball field with bleachers

For Dining: 6 picnic tables

For Kids: Playground, bike racks

Description: Flat, with sparse grass. Shade around the edges of the park. Partly fenced. Not a very appealing neighborhood.

Of Note: This one is really just a softball field and a swing set.

Walk 76: Backesto Park

Location: Jackson and 15th streets—easy to find. See Map 9.

Size: 10.47 acres, about half open grass

Parking: Neighborhood street parking

For Comfort: Restrooms on both sides of the park, near bocce courts and playground, clean, with wheelchair access; water fountains

For Sports: 8 tennis courts, 3 bocce ball courts, 4 handball courts, basketball courts, lighted softball field

For Dining: 11 picnic tables, 4 barbecues, one large barbecue

For Kids: Playground, bike racks

Description: Flat, with good grass. Beautiful shade trees. Quiet neighborhood. Unfenced. When I visited, lots of kids were using the park, but it was school vacation, so it may be quieter at other times.

Of Note: A pleasant open park in a nice neighborhood. It might be interesting to watch bocce ball being played.

Walk 77: Watson Park

Location: Jackson Street and Monferino Drive—a little hard to find. See Map 9.

Size: 29.30 acres, mostly soccer fields and natural area at edges

Parking: Lots on 22nd and on Jackson

For Comfort: Restrooms with wheelchair access, reasonably clean; water fountains

For Sports: 3 soccer fields, basketball courts, bleachers, lockers

For Dining: 16 picnic tables, 3 barbecues

For Kids: Playground

Description: Hill down from street to flat playing fields. A nice amount of shade. Good grass. Dirt path along part of stagnant creek, with unsightly dump at end. Lots of bird song. Some traffic noise from 101.

Of Note: A large park that can provide a good walk around the perimeter if you don't mind skirting the dump.

Walk 78: Roosevelt Park and Center

Location: 21st Street off Santa Clara Street—easy to find. See Map 9.

Size: 10.80 acres, about three-quarters open grass

Parking: Lots off 21st and on 20th

For Comfort: Restrooms with wheelchair access, reasonably clean; water fountain

For Sports: 2 tennis courts, basketball courts, softball field, soccer field

For Dining: 22 picnic tables, 5 barbecues, large barbecue pit

For Kids: Playground, bike racks

Description: Flat on playing fields, slightly rolling in front. Some traffic noise from Santa Clara. Landscaping around Community Center. Paved, lighted path running across the front.

Of Note: The section along Santa Clara in front of the Community Center is very attractive and inviting. The playing fields are rather rundown, with a desolate feeling.

Walk 79: Plata Arroyo Park

Location: King Road at Mabury—easy to find. See Map 9.

Size: 10.60 acres, nearly all open space

Parking: Neighborhood street parking

For Comfort: Water fountains

For Dining: 17 picnic tables, 17 barbecues

For Kids: Playground

Description: Rolling terrain with nice grass. A littered creek runs along the slanting side, and the ground at that side is muddy in spots. A short paved path leads to the pedestrian bridge over the creek. Not much shade. A small area of landscaping at the front.

Of Note: Although this is a fair-sized park, its shape makes it seem smaller than it is. It seems to be mostly a convenient pedestrian route through the area.

Walk 80: Emma Prusch Memorial Park

Location: King Road at Story Road—easy to find. See Map 9.

Size: 41.50 acres, about one-third open grass

Parking: Large lot off King

For Comfort: Restrooms with wheelchair access, very clean; water fountains

For Dining: Group picnic area

For Kids: (Of all ages) small and large domestic animals

Description: Beautifully landscaped rolling grounds, with antique farm equipment scattered about. Large area of open grass in the middle. Paved paths leading around and through, with decorative lights. Areas of interest include the Rare Fruit Orchard, old farmhouse, small-animal area, barn with large animals, International Grove, Leaf Bank (where leaves brought in from the neighborhood are composted), and Cornucopia and El Jardin community gardens. An Arts Center is under construction.

Of Note: If your dog doesn't lose control around farm animals, this is a fascinating place to bring him, because all the animals are out in plain sight and approachable.

Walk 81: Olinder-Martin Park

Location: Jeanne Avenue off Melbourne Blvd.—hard to find. See Map 9.

Size: 9.34 acres

Parking: Neighborhood street parking

Description: This is actually a flat vacant lot behind cyclone fencing, backing onto a railroad yard. It offers no entry and no reason to want to gain admittance.

Walk 82: William Street Park

Location: William Street at 16th Street—easy to find. See Map 9.

Size: 15.88 acres, nearly all open space

Parking: Lot at smaller section of park, street parking

For Comfort: Water fountains

For Dining: 23 picnic tables, 4 barbecues

For Kids: Playground, bike racks

Description: Flat, with nice grass; dirt areas under trees and around picnic tables. Dirt along top of creek bank. Pedestrian walkway over creek to connect large and small sections of park. Quiet. Some neighborhood dogs running loose.

Of Note: This is a nice large park with lovely trees, and a good balance of sun and shade. The creek is stagnant and scummy, but offers your dog interesting sights and sounds.

Walk 83: Kelley Park

Location: Senter Road between Keyes Street and Tully Road. See Map 9.

Size: 155.78 acres

Parking: Parking lot off Senter; no access from Roberts Avenue along back side of park

For Comfort: Restrooms, with wheelchair access, nice and clean; water fountains

For Dining: 75 tables, 47 barbecues, mostly in group picnic areas which can be reserved (call 277-5351)

For Kids: Happy Hollow play area and zoo, miniature train

Description: Slightly hilly, grass and natural areas. Lots of attractive shade trees of various types. Two loop paved paths from parking lot, one going past Japanese Friendship Garden and turning around at Historical Museum, the other winding more along railroad tracks and creek. Going toward the Historical Museum first, you can walk both loops without retracing your steps, for a total distance of about ¾ mile.

Of Note: Dogs are not allowed in Happy Hollow, the Japanese Friendship Garden, or the Historical Museum. But on a weekend morning in winter, I was the only one on the paths, and my dog was intensely interested in all the sights and sounds and smells.

Walk 84: Mayfair Park

Location: Kammerer Avenue off King Road—easy to find. See Map 10.

Size: 8.46 acres, hardly any open grass

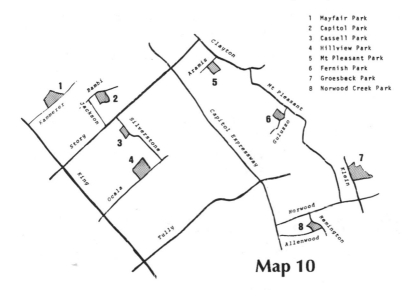

1 Mayfair Park
2 Capitol Park
3 Cassell Park
4 Hillview Park
5 Mt Pleasant Park
6 Fernish Park
7 Groesbeck Park
8 Norwood Creek Park

Map 10

Parking:	Neighborhood street parking
For Comfort:	Water fountain
For Sports:	Basketball courts
For Dining:	2 picnic tables, 2 barbecues
For Kids:	Playground
Description:	Flat, with most of the area taken up by an immense and obviously highly productive community garden. Some shade. Quiet.
Of Note:	Most of this park is actually the community garden, leaving little space for you and your dog to romp.

Walk 85: Capitol Park

Location:	Bambi Lane off Jackson Avenue—slightly hard to find. See Map 10.
Size:	11.63 acres, nearly all open grass
Parking:	Neighborhood street parking
For Comfort:	Restrooms with wheelchair access, clean; water fountain

For Sports:	3 tennis courts, softball field with bleachers, soccer field with bleachers
For Dining:	9 picnic tables, 3 barbecues
For Kids:	Playground
Description:	Mostly flat, with good lush grass. Beautiful shade trees scattered through park. Several picnic areas. Unfenced. Paved lighted path across. Quiet.
Of Note:	This park has a very pleasant air about it, and provides a nice walk around the perimeter.

Walk 86: Sylvia Cassell Park

Location:	Leeward Drive off Story Road—easy to find. See Map 10.
Size:	1.40 acres, all open
Parking:	Neighborhood street parking
Description:	Undeveloped. This is really just an empty lot running along the road, with plenty of broken glass littering its weeds. If I were Sylvia Cassell, I'd be truly dismayed to have this patch named after me.

Walk 87: Hillview Park

Location:	Ocala Avenue and Berona Way—easy to find. See Map 10.
Size:	14.80 acres, nearly all open grass
Parking:	Lot on Ocala, neighborhood street parking
For Comfort:	Restrooms, with wheelchair access, reasonably clean; water fountain
For Sports:	Softball field with bleachers, soccer field
For Dining:	7 picnic tables, 2 barbecues
For Kids:	Playground, bike racks

Description:	Rolling land with nice grass. Some good areas of shade. Small planes buzzing overhead most of the time, otherwise quiet. Unfenced.
Of Note:	If you like to watch small planes, this is the park for you, situated right at the end of the runway for Reid Hillview Airport.

Walk 88: Mount Pleasant Park

Location:	Aramis Drive off Clayton Road—a little hard to find. See Map 10.
Size:	5.44 acres, more than three-quarters open grass
Parking:	Neighborhood street parking
For Comfort:	Water fountain
For Sports:	Tennis courts, basketball courts
For Dining:	6 picnic tables, 3 barbecues
For Kids:	Playground
Description:	Slightly rolling, with good grass. Good shade areas. Paved path across one corner. Some small-airplane noise.
Of Note:	Although this seems to be a nice quiet neighborhood, the park has obviously suffered from vandalism. The tennis courts are chained shut with a San Jose Police Department NO TRESPASSING sign, and the tire swings are missing from their supports in the playground.

Walk 89: Fernish Park

Location:	Guluzzo Drive off Mt. Pleasant Road—a little hard to find. See Map 10.
Size:	5.98 acres, nearly all open grass
Parking:	Neighborhood street parking
For Comfort:	Water fountain

For Sports:	4-station parcourse
For Dining:	6 picnic tables, 6 barbecues
For Kids:	Playground
Description:	Hilly, with nice grass. A lovely huge area of shade runs across the middle of the park. Picnic tables are scattered under the trees. Benches around the playground, which includes a merry-go-round with horses to ride. Unfenced. Quiet.
Of Note:	It's hard to tell where the park ends and the adjacent school yard begins. Between them, this one offers considerable open space.

Walk 90: Groesbeck Hill Park

Location:	Klein Road off Murillo Avenue—hard to find. See Map 10.
Size:	26.61 acres, all open land
Parking:	Neighborhood street parking
Description:	Undeveloped. This is a fenced green hillside that looks as if it's kept plowed. On it is a barn overflowing with hay. There is no access.
Of Note:	This is a big sloping area of open space, and if ever converted to a park could be a really nice one. If you are interested in future plans for this land, check with the San Jose Parks and Recreation Department.

Walk 91: Norwood Creek Park

Location:	Centerwood Way off Remington Way—hard to find. See Map 10.
Size:	5 acres, maybe half open grass
Parking:	Neighborhood street parking
For Comfort:	Water fountains at back of school
For Sports:	Parcourse, softball field, soccer field

For Kids: Playground at school

Description: Slightly rolling, with somewhat sparse grass. No shade. Garbage thrown into the side of the park facing the road.

Of Note: Most of the space is actually taken up by Norwood Creek Elementary School. This one isn't worth finding.

Walk 92: North Coyote Park

Location: On Old Oakland Road near Murphy—easy to find. See Map 11.

Size: About 9 acres, all open space

Parking: Street

Description: Undeveloped. Stretch along a creek, with trees lining the bank and a dirt path running along it.

Of Note: Currently, this is not worth a visit. If you are interested in plans for the area, contact the San Jose Parks and Recreation Department.

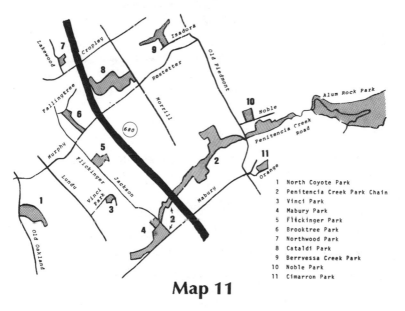

1   North Coyote Park
2   Penitencia Creek Park Chain
3   Vinci Park
4   Mabury Park
5   Flickinger Park
6   Brooktree Park
7   Northwood Park
8   Cataldi Park
9   Berryessa Creek Park
10   Noble Park
11   Cimarron Park

Map 11

Walk 93: Penitencia Creek Park Chain

Location: Jackson Avenue, Pentencia Creek Road—easy to find. See Map 11.

Size: 24.32 acres, nearly all open grass or dirt

Parking: Lot on Jackson, lot on Penitencia Creek

For Dining: 10 picnic tables scattered through section along Jackson Avenue

Description: This is actually several parks, some connected, some not, running along Penitencia Creek. The section at Jackson is large and mostly flat. There are paved paths snaking through and across the park. The creek is live and accessible. There are lots of animal burrows.

The section running along the south side of Penitencia Creek Road is somewhat weedy and wild, with a path paralleling the road.

When the park changes to the north side of the road, it again opens out into a large area. The creek runs along the road, and a dirt path leads along the creek. Paved paths wind across the park and to a fenced pond with egrets, coots, ducks and gulls. The final section past Noble Park is fenced with NO TRESPASSING signs.

Of Note: The Jackson Avenue section is the nicest place to actually reach the creek, which is an attractive little stream. The large section north of Penitencia Creek Road is a great place to follow the paths and watch the waterbirds.

Walk 94: Vinci Park

Location: Vinci Park Way off Berryessa Road. See Map 11.

Size: 3 acres, nearly all open grass

Parking: Neighborhood street parking

For Comfort: Water fountain

For Sports: Soccer field, overgrown parcourse

For Dining: 9 picnic tables, 6 barbecues

For Kids: Playground

Description:	Slightly rolling, with weedy but thick grass. Some landscaping. Paved lighted path across park. Quiet.
Of Note:	This is a small but attractive park, with interesting playground equipment at the adjacent school.

Walk 95: Mabury Park

Location:	Commodore Drive and Jackson Avenue—easy to find. See Map 11.
Size:	3 acres, all open space
Parking:	Neighborhood street parking
Description:	Undeveloped. Actually just a hilly grass lot that backs up against Penitencia Creek.
Of Note:	Unless for some reason you want to visit the creek from the other side, continue down Jackson and park in the lot for this section of the Penitencia Creek Park chain.

Walk 96: Flickinger Park

Location:	Flickinger Avenue—easy to find. See Map 11.
Size:	14.41 acres, about half open grass
Parking:	Lot on Ulster Drive, street parking on Flickinger
For Sports:	2 softball fields with bleachers and fences, soccer field, basketball courts, 8 chess tables
For Comfort:	Restrooms with wheelchair access, in reasonably clean condition; water fountains
For Dining:	15 picnic tables, 4 barbecues
For Kids:	Playground, bike racks
Description:	Mostly flat, with good grass. Absolutely no shade. Some traffic noise from Flickinger. In use by lots of sports enthusiasts. Snack bar area in the building with the restrooms, but closed up tight on my visit.
Of Note:	This is a park for organized athletics, and it is well used for that purpose.

Walk 97: Brooktree Park

Location: Shadetree Lane off Coraltree Place—a little hard to find. See Map 11.

Size: 7.67 acres, nearly all open grass

Parking: Neighborhood street parking

For Comfort: Water fountain

For Sports: Soccer field

For Dining: 10 picnic tables, 4 barbecues

Description: Flat, with nice grass and some areas of shade. Paved lighted path across one end. Unfenced. Quiet. The "neck" section shown on maps is actually a fenced vacant lot under high powerlines, not yet developed into anything parklike.

Of Note: This one backs on a school of interesting architectural design, seeming to rise out of the ground.

Walk 98: Northwood Park

Location: Lakewood Drive off Cropley Avenue—a little hard to find. See Map 11.

Size: 4 acres, nearly all open grass

Parking: Neighborhood street parking

For Comfort: Water fountains

For Dining: 6 picnic tables, 2 barbecues

For Kids: Playground

Description: Slightly rolling, with nice grass. Shade only at one end in a dirt area. Paved, lighted path curving across length and width of park. Quiet. Unfenced.

Of Note: A huge merry-go-round with tires suspended from massive wooden arms looks like a lot of fun, but needs a crowd to really get it going.

Walk 99: Cataldi Park

Location:	Morrill Avenue at Cataldi Drive—easy to find. See Map 11.
Size:	33.52 acres, about three-quarters open grass
Parking:	Lot on Cataldi, street parking on Morrill
For Comfort:	Restrooms with wheelchair access, in good condition; water fountains
For Sports:	Parcourse, soccer field, 4 tennis courts
For Dining:	18 tables, 2 barbecues
For Kids:	Playground
Description:	Mostly flat, with a couple of small hills. Grass a bit sparse in places. Paved lighted path winding along Cataldi side. Unfenced. Quiet but popular.
Of Note:	Because of the park's irregular shape and large size, a walk around the perimeter offers quite a workout, especially if you run the parcourse along your way.

Walk 100: Berryessa Creek Park

Location: Messina Drive off Knightsbridge Road—a little hard to find. See Map 11.

Size: 13.69 acres, nearly all open grass or dirt

Parking: Neighborhood street parking

For Comfort: Water fountain

For Sports: Basketball courts, softball field

For Dining: 7 picnic tables, 3 barbecues

For Kids: Playground

Description: Mostly flat, rising slightly to dirt levee along creekbed (dry at present). Grass is okay, but very little shade. Unfenced. Paved path across.

Of Note: This could be a very pleasant and quiet park, but on my visits we were faced with an obnoxious and extremely loud three-wheel off-road vehicle tearing up and down the levee, and local dogs rushing out at us.

Walk 101: Noble Park

Location: Noble Avenue off Old Piedmont Road—easy to find. See Map 11.

Size: 8.40 acres, nearly all open grass

Parking: Lot off Noble, shared with library

For Comfort: Restrooms with wheelchair access, nice and clean; water fountain

For Sports: Softball field at adjacent school

For Dining: 5 picnic tables

For Kids: Playground

Description: Little rolling hills with good grass. Plenty of shade. Wading pond about one to one and a half feet deep. Picnic tables placed singly under the trees. Quiet.

Of Note: The wading pond is a nice place to cool feet, both yours and your dog's.

Walk 102: Cimarron Park

Location: Orange and Pride streets—a little hard to find. See Map 11.

Size: 7.20 acres, nearly all open grass

Parking: Neighborhood street parking

For Comfort: Water fountain

For Sports: Basketball courts

For Dining: 7 picnic tables

For Kids: Playground

Description: Rolling, with good grass. Paved, lighted path winding across. Unfenced. Quiet neighborhood.

Of Note: This is a pleasant plot of green—seeming smaller than it actually is—and nice if you happen to live nearby. There's nothing special to recommend it if you have to travel to it.

Walk 103: Alviso Marina

Location: End of Elizabeth Street—if you can find Alviso, you can find the marina. See Map 12.

Size: Unknown

Parking: Lot at the marina

For Comfort: Restrooms, not too clean; water fountain

For Sports: Fishing

For Dining: 3 picnic tables

Description: The marina sits at the edge of the San Francisco Bay National Wildlife Refuge. Alviso Slough Trail leads into the Refuge where dogs are not allowed. At the opposite end of the marina is a trail on a levee that loops around a weedy area holding picnic tables, and along an arm of the slough.

Of Note: Alviso is an odd little area, part of San Jose, yet more a community in itself. It's not worth coming here for the marina and the park, but there is an interesting mural, some nice Victorians, and picturesque old boats.

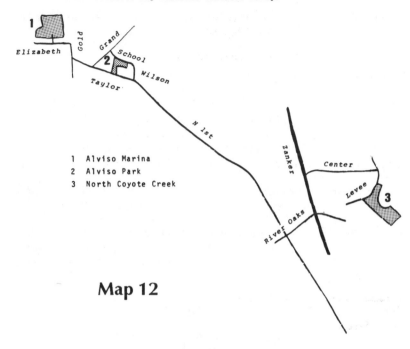

San Francisco Bay National Wildlife Refuge

1   Alviso Marina
2   Alviso Park
3   North Coyote Creek

Map 12

Walk 104: Alviso Park

Location:	School Street off Taylor Street—easy to find. See Map 12.
Size:	7.49 acres, mostly open grass
Parking:	Neighborhood street parking
For Comfort:	Restrooms, not too clean; water fountain.
For Sports:	Swimming pool, softball field
For Dining:	10 picnic tables, 3 barbecues
For Kids:	Playground
Description:	Mostly flat. The grass is being allowed to die because of the drought. Primitive playground. Some shade. Airplane noise overhead at times.
Of Note:	Unless you are coming to Alviso for some particular reason, the park is definitely not worth the drive.

Walk 105: North Coyote Creek Park

Location: Off Zanker Road, behind Agnews Hospital—hard to find. See Map 12.

Size: About 10 acres, all open space

Parking: Street

Description: First you have to make your way through Agnews Hospital, then you find that the road into the parksite area is marked with a NO TRESPASSING sign. If you ignore that and continue on, you will find a sort of summer camp for the children at Agnews, but no park.

Of Note: If plans are in the works for development of this site, the access will probably change. The roads around Agnews were under construction when I visited, so perhaps change is already underway.

Dogs Are Not Welcome At:

San Jose

Almaden Lake—the beach and swim area

Alum Rock Park

Golf Course on Old Oakland Highway

Kelley Park—Happy Hollow, the Historical Museum, the Japanese Friendship Garden, and Leninger Center

Lake Cunningham Park

Municipal Stadium

Overfelt Botanical Garden

PAL Sports Center

Rose Garden

Almaden Quicksilver County Park—except for Senator Mine area

Hellyer County Park—except for Claitor area

Santa Teresa County Park—golf course

Calero Reservoir

Part Two
The Rest of
Santa Clara County

The rest of the county is broken into a dozen small cities and unincorporated lands. Taken together, they cover approximately the same area as San Jose, and have about the same number and variety of parks. As this is being written, two of the county's cities are struggling with the issue of retaining a reminder of their agricultural past by saving the last orchards standing within their boundaries. On a larger scale, the November 1990 election included an opportunity to create a South Bay Open Space District, modeled after the successful Midpeninsula Open Space District. Although the measure failed to receive the required two-thirds majority, it came very close, and will undoubtedly appear on the next ballot for another try.

Of the cities in Santa Clara County, only one still maintains a "no dogs allowed" policy in its parks. That city is Campbell, and thus far pleas to the recreation department to change its stance have fallen on deaf and unfriendly ears. Fortunately, there are a county park and the multiple-jurisdiction Los Gatos Creek Trail within the city, so there are places dog owners can go. But driving by an empty park on a winter's day and knowing you can't set foot in it with your dog continues to be an annoyance.

Los Altos is nearly as bad. Although there is no city-wide ordinance prohibiting dogs in parks, the parks are individually signed and most of them don't allow dogs. Only one park of any size or interest is open to those who wish to bring their dogs. Nearby Los Altos Hills has only one park, but it's a beauty and dogs are permitted. Los Altos residents may want to avail themselves of that park or the Foothill College campus.

The remaining cities—Milpitas, Santa Clara, Los Gatos, Saratoga, Sunnyvale, Cupertino, Mountain View and Palo Alto—all require that dogs be on a six-foot leash and that their owners clean up after them. The Midpeninsula Open Space District varies its regulations on a preserve-by-preserve basis. Those preserves where dogs are allowed are covered in this chapter.

All in all, Santa Clara County is gifted with hundreds of excellent parks and a friendly, dogs-allowed, attitude. Each town's section begins with an introduction and a map. Park descriptions follow in the same order in which they are listed on the map. Areas where dogs are not welcome are listed at the end of the chapter for all towns and districts.

Chapter 1
Milpitas

Milpitas has a lot of parks for a city its size, and all are open to dogs. The usual leash and pooper-scooper laws apply.

A plan unique to Milpitas seems to be to connect parks where possible. So instead of visiting just one park, you can start in one, meander to another, and maybe even a third, and have a nice walk and a variety of scenery. Murphy, Yellowstone and Sinnott parks are all connected, as are Peter D. Gill and Walter Reuther. If you like Spanish architecture, you should find Higuera Adobe particularly appealing.

The majority of Milpitas parks are clean and well maintained, but a few show signs of litter and vandalism problems. The problem areas are noted in the individual park descriptions.

Walk 1: Pinewood Park

Location: Lonetree Court off Fallen Leaf Drive—a little hard to find. See Map 13.

Size: 8 acres, nearly all open grass

Parking: Neighborhood street parking

For Comfort: Restrooms, reasonably clean; water fountain

For Sports: 4 lighted tennis courts, basketball court

For Dining: 4 picnic tables, 2 barbecues

For Kids: 3 playgrounds

Description: Mostly flat, with a couple of small knolls. Nice grass and good shade areas. Lighted, paved path around perimeter. Olive trees in one area, with olives all over the ground in season.

Of Note: There is broken glass along much of the path, but otherwise this is an attractive park. The play area tucked into one side spur of the park has a sway bridge.

MILPITAS

1	Pinewood Park
2	Starlite Park
3	Hall Memorial Park
4	Hidden Lake Park
5	Peter Gill Memorial Park
6	Strickroth Park
7	Reuther Park
8	Sandalwood Park
9	Sunnyhills Park
10	Higuera Adobe Park
11	Calle Oriente Mini Park
12	Cardoza Park
13	Foothill Park
14	Ben Rodgers Park
15	Murphy Park
16	Yellowstone Park
17	Sinnott Park
18	Creighton Park

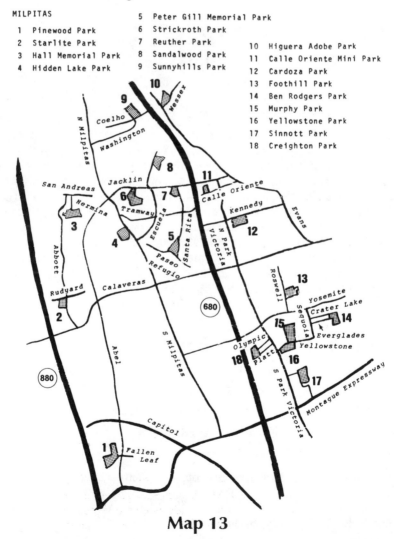

Map 13

Walk 2: Starlite Park

Location:	Abbott Avenue at Rudyard Drive—easy to find. See Map 13.
Size:	4 acres, mostly open grass
Parking:	Neighborhood street parking
For Comfort:	Restrooms, somewhat dirty; water fountain was not functioning on my visit
For Sports:	Horseshoe pits
For Dining:	5 picnic tables, 4 barbecues
For Kids:	Playground
Description:	Slightly rolling, with grass in the middle and dirt under the trees around the edges. Good shade. Dirt path leads around three sides. An unusual cactus structure sits in a circle by itself. There is some traffic noise, and some evidence of vandalism.
Of Note:	There is some broken glass on the path and hidden in the grass. Somehow this park seems smaller than 4 acres. There are larger, more appealing parks nearby.

Walk 3: Hall Memorial Park

Location:	Hermina Street off San Andreas Drive—hard to find. See Map 13.
Size:	9.5 acres, mostly either grass or water
Parking:	Lot with 18 spaces at end of Hermina
For Comfort:	Restrooms, nice and clean; water fountain
For Sports:	4 tennis courts, lighted soccer field
For Dining:	6 picnic tables, 2 barbecues
For Kids:	2 playgrounds
Description:	Mostly flat, with attractive arched bridges over a pond and canal. Pond is fenced and no swimming is allowed. Not much shade available. Actually, this is a small park of mostly water, connected to a larger park

of mostly grass by the bridges. A paved path runs across both sections.

Of Note: The pond is actually fenced only part way around, and you can walk along the water if it hasn't been raining recently.

Walk 4: Hidden Lake Park

Location: North Milpitas Blvd. north of Escuela Drive—easy to find. See Map 13.

Size: 1.5 acres, nearly all water

Parking: Lot with 15 spaces off Milpitas

For Sports: Model boats permitted

For Dining: 9 picnic tables, 2 barbecues

Description: Flat area surrounding large pond with ducks, coots and seagulls. Paved path leads around. Picnic tables are spaced out along path. No shade anywhere. Dock leads out over water.

Of Note: As long as it's not too hot, this is a fun place to ramble around the pond and have lunch while you watch and share with the ducks.

Walk 5: Peter D. Gill Memorial Park

Location: Paseo Refugio off Hillview Drive—easy to find. See Map 13.

Size: 5.5 acres, about half open grass

Parking: Lot with 20 spaces off Santa Rita

For Comfort: Restrooms, in clean condition; water fountain

For Sports: 3 tennis courts, 2 half courts, lighted fenced softball field with bleachers, basketball court, parcourse

For Dining: 8 picnic tables, 4 barbecues

For Kids: Playground

Description:	Mostly flat, with good grass. No shade anywhere. Well-used, even on a winter weekday. Fairly quiet.
Of Note:	A dirt path continues north out of the park past Tramway, for about ½ mile. You can connect with the dirt path to Reuther Park by walking a short distance along Santa Rita Road. It's a ¼-mile wide dirt path on the right.

Walk 6: Strickroth Park

Location:	Clauser Drive off Escuela Drive off Jacklin Road—easy to find. See Map 13.
Size:	5.7 acres, nearly all open
Parking:	Neighborhood street parking
For Comfort:	Water fountain was not functioning on my visit
For Sports:	Softball field
For Dining:	6 picnic tables, 2 barbecues
For Kids:	Sand areas where playgrounds probably once were, but nothing there now
Description:	Rolling terrain with nice grass. Large sunny area. Scattered shade trees. Some traffic noise.
Of Note:	Considering the removal of the playground equipment and a nonfunctioning fountain, this seems to be a park on the way down at the moment. Perhaps there are plans for rehabilitation.

Walk 7: Walter Reuther Park

Location:	Jacklin Road—easy to find. See Map 13.
Size:	5.2 acres, nearly all open
Parking:	Neighborhood street parking
For Comfort:	Water fountain
For Sports:	Parcourse
For Dining:	5 picnic tables, 2 barbecues

For Kids:	Playground
Description:	Mostly flat, with nice grass. Some limited shade. Traffic noise from Jacklin. Dirt path leads down one side, with parcourse along it.
Of Note:	From the road, the park looks small. But the dirt path continues south out the back of the park for approximately ¼ mile before coming out on Santa Rita. A little way down Santa Rita you can start on the dirt path that leads into Peter D. Gill Memorial Park.

Walk 8: Sandalwood Park

Location:	Escuela Parkway at Russell Lane—easy to find. See Map 13.
Size:	1.5 acres, mostly open
Parking:	Neighborhood street parking, not directly adjacent to park
For Comfort:	Water fountains
For Sports:	Horseshoe pits
For Dining:	4 picnic tables, 3 barbecues
For Kids:	Playground
Description:	Flat, with some limited shade.
Of Note:	This is really just a pocketbook-size piece of lawn, and if you don't happen to live nearby, there's no reason to come.

Walk 9: Sunnyhills Park

Location:	Coelho Street off Arizona Avenue—easy to find. See Map 13.
Size:	6 acres, nearly all open grass
Parking:	Neighborhood street parking
For Comfort:	Restrooms, in okay condition; water fountain
For Dining:	10 picnic tables, 4 barbecues

For Kids:	Playground
Description:	Slightly rolling, with very nice grass. Lots of shade. Paved path runs across length. Quiet. Playground is lighted. Very clean.
Of Note:	The park is very attractive, with lovely great shade trees and just enough landscaping to make it pretty. The playground equipment offers lots of fun for both kids and dogs.

Walk 10: Higuera Adobe Park

Location:	Wessex Place off North Park Victoria Drive—easy to find, with signs along the way. See Map 13.
Size:	5.5 acres, all open
Parking:	Lot with 20 spaces off Wessex
For Comfort:	Water fountain
For Dining:	11 picnic tables, 7 barbecues
For Kids:	Playground

Description:	Flat lawn area runs back to strip of natural area, mostly shaded, along dry creekbed. Park backs up to fenced vacant hills. Seems to be a very popular place with birds, and there's lots of bird song. Unfortunately, there's also lots of traffic noise from nearby 680.
Of Note:	The old adobe is extremely attractive, sparkling white, with red-tile roof and wrought-iron window guards.

Walk 11: Calle Oriente Mini Park

Location:	Calle Oriente off North Park Victoria Drive—easy to find. See Map 13.
Size:	2 acres, nearly all paved
Parking:	Neighborhood street parking
For Sports:	Basketball court, 2 handball courts
For Dining:	2 picnic tables
For Kids:	Playground
Description:	A sand playground area, otherwise paved.
Of Note:	This is really just a playground and a basketball court, and doesn't have much to offer you and your dog.

Walk 12: Cardoza Park

Location:	Kennedy Drive off North Park Victoria Drive—easy to find. See Map 13.
Size:	10 acres, about three-quarters open grass
Parking:	2 lots along Kennedy, each with 25 spaces
For Comfort:	Restrooms, reasonably clean; water fountain
For Sports:	Horseshoe pits, 2 lighted softball fields, basketball hoop in one parking lot
For Dining:	20 picnic tables, 6 regular barbecues, 2 large group barbecues

For Kids: 2 playgrounds

Description: Slightly rolling, with nice grass. Some limited shade. Softball fields and one of the playgrounds are fenced off, but accessible. Dirt path runs around main section of the park and is lighted. An outdoor amphitheater made of rock is situated near the group picnic area.

Of Note: The playgrounds are different and interesting: one has tires hung from a post which you can try to coax your dog to jump through and the other has large rocks and stone pilings of various heights.

Walk 13: Foothill Park

Location: Roswell Drive off Yosemite Drive—easy to find. See Map 13.

Size: 4 acres, nearly all open grass

Parking: Neighborhood street parking

For Comfort: Restrooms with wheelchair access, reasonably clean; water fountains

For Dining: 4 picnic tables, 3 barbecues

For Kids: Playground

Description: Mostly flat with a few small rises. Good sun areas and nice patches of shade. Lighted dirt path through the length of the park. Quiet.

Of Note: This park has a rather nice private but open feel to it, maybe because of fences and shade on three sides and a large, open playing field on the fourth.

Walk 14: Ben Rodgers Park

Location: Everglades Drive or Grand Teton Drive off Sequoia Drive—easy to find. See Map 13.

Size: 5 acres, nearly all open grass

Parking: Neighborhood street parking

For Comfort: Water fountain

For Dining: 4 picnic tables, 2 barbecues

For Kids: Playground.

Description: Sloping terrain, mostly open grass, with landscaping around the perimeter. Small areas of shade under mostly pine trees. Quiet. Fenced along neighbors' back yards. Gravel trail around most of circumference.

Of Note: This is an irregularly shaped park, and the path makes for a nice walk. Many of Milpitas' parks seem to be used by people playing sports, so this one has a better chance of being empty.

Walk 15: Murphy Park

Location: Yellowstone Avenue off South Park Victoria Drive— easy to find. See Map 13.

Size: 8.7 acres, nearly all open grass

Parking: Lot with 18 spaces off Yellowstone

For Comfort: Restrooms, reasonably clean; water fountain

For Sports: Parcourse, which continues through Yellowstone Park and on into Sinnott Park; soccer field

For Dining: 6 picnic tables, 1 barbecue

For Kids: Playground

Description: Flat on the soccer field, rolling hills in most of the rest. Good grass, and well lighted. Paved path runs around perimeter up to soccer field and across park's width in several places. Some patches of shade. Quiet.

Of Note: Murphy Park, Yellowstone Park and Sinnott Park actually all connect via paved paths, and make for quite an extensive and interesting ramble.

Walk 16: Yellowstone Park

Location: Yellowstone Avenue and South Park Victoria Drive—easy to find. See Map 13.

Size: 4 acres, about three-quarters open grass

Parking: Neighborhood street parking or in the lot for Murphy Park across the street

For Comfort: Water fountain

For Sports: 4 lighted tennis courts, parcourse that continues on one side into Murphy Park and on the other into Sinnott Park

Description: Mostly flat; nice grass with a paved path around. Shade and benches at corner at Park Victoria and behind tennis courts. Nice landscaping. Lights generally throughout park.

Of Note: It's hard to tell where Yellowstone Park ends and the adjacent school begins. There's a lighted softball field that probably belongs to the school. There was some glass along the edge of the paved path leading to Sinnott Park, but not on the path itself.

Walk 17: Sinnott Park

Location:	Clear Lake Avenue off South Park Victoria Drive—easy to find. See Map 13.
Size:	4.7 acres, mostly open grass
Parking:	Neighborhood street parking
For Comfort:	Restrooms, reasonably clean; water fountain
For Sports:	Parcourse, running into and through Yellowstone Park and into Murphy Park
For Dining:	3 picnic tables, 1 barbecue
For Kids:	Playground
Description:	Huge sand area around the playground; otherwise, flat grass area. Nice shade trees down the middle of the park and in one corner.
Of Note:	The gravel path along the parcourse becomes a paved path and leads through Yellowstone Park and across the street to Murphy Park.

Walk 18: Creighton Park

Location:	Olympic Drive off South Park Victoria Drive—easy to find. See Map 13.
Size:	5 acres, nearly all open grass
Parking:	Neighborhood street parking
For Comfort:	Water fountain
For Dining:	10 picnic tables, 5 barbecues
For Kids:	Playground
Description:	Mostly flat, with some ivy and shrubs for landscaping. Small trees are attractive, but don't provide much shade. A dirt path runs around the park, with picnic tables scattered along it. Fenced on one side along neighbors' back yards. Traffic noise.
Of Note:	If some traffic noise doesn't bother you, this is a nice sunny park for cooler days.

Chapter 2
Santa Clara

It is obvious that at one time dogs were not welcome in Santa Clara's parks. Park visitors are greeted with a large sign proclaiming NO DOGS ALLOWED and a smaller sign tucked underneath amending it to EXCEPT ON 6 FOOT LEASH. Congratulations to the Santa Clara city fathers on their enlightenment. These days they have only the usual leash and pooper-scooper laws.

There are some unusual facilities in parks in Santa Clara. Many contain buildings consisting of two rooms separated by a central patio. They can be reserved through the recreation department, and are used by such people as the Girl Scouts, day-care groups, and 4-H'ers training guide dogs.

Restrooms are present but not always accessible in Santa Clara. Although facilities exist in each park, in times of low usage they are kept locked. This means that on a winter weekday, only the popular Central Park may have unlocked facilities. On winter weekends, most are unlocked, and during the summer only in those few parks where vandalism is a problem are restrooms kept locked. The notation "(locked)" after restrooms in the park writeups refers to their condition when I visited on a winter day.

Santa Clara parks are generally well planned and well maintained, and a pleasure to visit.

Walk 1: Westwood Oaks Park

Location: La Herran Drive off Pruneridge Avenue—easy to find. See Map 14.

Size: 1 acre, mostly open grass

Parking: Neighborhood street parking

For Comfort: Restrooms (locked); water fountain

For Sports: Basketball court

For Dining: 1 picnic table, 1 barbecue

For Kids: Playground, bike racks

Description: Flat except for two small mounds. Grass mostly parched. Lighted, paved path around perimeter. Good areas of shade. Fenced except on street side. Quiet. Two-room building, one room used as day-care center.

Of Note: This is a smallish park, and unless you live nearby, there's no reason to come here rather than one of the other, larger parks.

Walk 2: Maywood Park

Location: Pruneridge Avenue—easy to find. See Map 14.

Size: 9.5 acres, nearly all open grass

Parking: Lot with 20 spaces off Pruneridge

For Comfort: Restrooms (locked); water fountain

For Sports: 2 tennis courts, softball field

For Dining: 16 picnic tables, 6 barbecues

For Kids: Playground, bike racks

Description: Mostly flat except for two or three small mounds. Lots of shade areas, with old interesting trees. Lighted path, partly paved, partly dirt, around most of perimeter. Concrete-lined creek running along one side of park. Busy school yard behind. Unfenced. Two-room building, used by, among others, 4-H to train guide dogs.

Of Note: This is a good-sized park with the odd shape of two triangles joined together. A walk completely around it is quite a nice ramble.

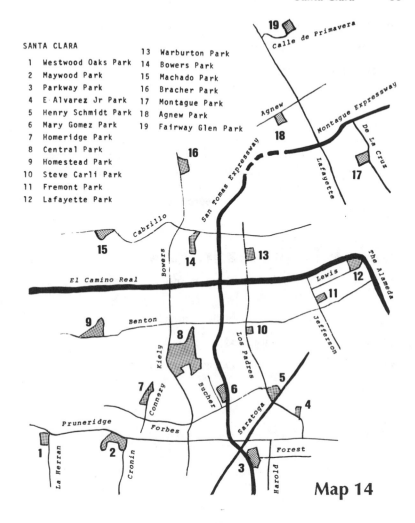

SANTA CLARA

1 Westwood Oaks Park
2 Maywood Park
3 Parkway Park
4 E Alvarez Jr Park
5 Henry Schmidt Park
6 Mary Gomez Park
7 Homeridge Park
8 Central Park
9 Homestead Park
10 Steve Carli Park
11 Fremont Park
12 Lafayette Park
13 Warburton Park
14 Bowers Park
15 Machado Park
16 Bracher Park
17 Montague Park
18 Agnew Park
19 Fairway Glen Park

Map 14

Walk 3: Parkway Park

Location: Forest Place off Cypress Avenue—rather hard to find, and access *only* at Forest. See Map 14.

Size: 3.5 acres, all open grass

Parking: Neighborhood street parking

For Comfort: Restrooms (locked)

For Sports: Parcourse

For Dining: 3 picnic tables, 3 barbecues

For Kids: Playground

Description: Sloping, rolling ground with mediocre grass. Good areas of shade. Paved path only in a small loop to the playground and pedestrian walkway over San Tomas Expressway. Traffic noise from San Tomas.

Of Note: The signs in Santa Clara parks give somewhat less than an open-armed welcome to dog owners, with NO DOGS ALLOWED featured prominently, and EXCEPT ON 6 FOOT LEASH in smaller, less obvious print. Still, dogs are indeed permitted.

Walk 4: E. Alvarez Jr. Park

Location: Los Padres Blvd. off Saratoga Avenue—easy to find. See Map 14.

Size: 3 acres, about two-thirds open grass

Parking: Neighborhood street parking

For Comfort: Restrooms (locked); water fountain

For Sports: Basketball hoop

For Dining: 2 picnic tables

For Kids: Playground, bike racks

Description: Slightly hilly, with some nice landscaping. Okay grass. Picnic tables located in pleasant area of shade. Paved path running across park. Large playground area. Quiet.

Of Note: This is a small but pleasant park, with a variety of types of trees adding visual interest.

Walk 5: Henry Schmidt Park

Location: Los Padres Blvd. and Saratoga Avenue—easy to find.
                   See Map 14.

Size: 8 acres, about three-quarters open grass

Parking: Lot with 20 spaces off Los Padres

For Comfort: Restrooms (locked); water fountain

For Sports: 4 tennis courts, parcourse around perimeter, softball
                   field, basketball court

For Dining: 5 picnic tables, 5 barbecues

For Kids: Playground with theme of train station

Description: Mostly flat, with a slight rolling hill in one section.
                   Acceptable grass. A nice blend of sun and shade.
                   Paved path winding across width. Quiet.

Of Note: The playground is a place of great photo opportuni-
                   ties, with a small-scale train engine and caboose, and
                   a same-size train station and water tower.

Walk 6: Mary Gomez Park

Location: Bucher Avenue off Forbes Avenue—easy to find. See Map 14.

Size: 8 acres, nearly all open

Parking: Lot with 20 spaces off Bucher Avenue

For Comfort: Restrooms in Swim Center Building, locked when pool is closed; water fountains

For Sports: Swimming pool, 2 tennis courts, basketball court

For Dining: 3 picnic tables, 3 barbecues at one end of park; 4 picnic tables, 2 barbecues at other end

For Kids: Playground

Description: Slightly rolling, with grass dying from lack of water. Nice shade areas. Paved path most of the way down length. Some traffic noise from San Tomas Expressway.

Of Note: Several small areas are tucked in around the tennis courts and swim center, screened off from the rest of the park, with a very private feel to them. The triangular patch of grass directly behind the tennis courts is extremely sheltered.

Walk 7: Homeridge Park

Location: Stevenson Street off Woodhams Road—easy to find. See Map 14.

Size: 6 acres, nearly all open grass

Parking: Lot with 15 spaces off Stevenson

For Comfort: Restrooms (locked), water fountain

For Sports: Basketball court

For Dining: Group area with 11 huge tables and 4 large barbecues; 16 individual tables and 6 barbecues

For Kids: Playground, bike racks

Description: Flat park with mostly shade. Much deeper than it looks from the street. Concrete-lined creek down one side. Paved path running through to Salem Drive. Fenced along the two long sides. Quiet.

Of Note: I was warned on my visit about a pack of dobermans running loose, and there were several dogs barking nearby, so use caution.

Walk 8: Central Park

Location: Kiely Blvd. between Homestead Road and Benton Street—easy to find. See Map 14.

Size: 52 acres, about three-quarters open grass

Parking: 2 large lots off Kiely, 1 large lot off Homestead or Patricia

For Comfort: Restrooms and fountains are located in several areas of the park

For Sports: International Swim Center (open even in winter); lawn bowling; parcourse; basketball courts; 2 lighted tennis courts; 2 lighted softball fields with bleachers

For Dining: 3 group areas under Pavilion; 3 group areas in Arbor Center; 16 individual picnic tables and 8 barbecues near Arbor Center

For Kids: 3 playgrounds, one with lots of tunnels, one fenced in with community center for tots

Description: Slightly rolling, with grass parched in the sunnier areas. Lighted, paved paths running all through park. Duck pond (no swimming or wading). Lots of sun and shade areas. Two arched wooden bridges over concrete-lined creek. Log amphitheater. Community center. Unfenced. Nice landscaping.

Of Note: Bundle up on a windy winter's day and come when the park is almost empty. There are plenty of birds and squirrels, and you may see Olympic swimmers training at the swim center.

Walk 9: Homestead Park

Location:	Benton Street off Lawrence Expwy.—easy to find. See Map 14.
Size:	10.5 acres, about half open grass
Parking:	Lot with 20 spaces off Benton
For Comfort:	Restrooms, clean; water fountains
For Sports:	2 lighted tennis courts, lighted basketball courts, fenced softball field with bleachers
For Dining:	Group area with 4 large tables and 1 large barbecue; 2 individual areas at opposite ends of park, one with 3 tables and 1 barbecue, the other with 4 tables and 4 barbecues
For Kids:	Playground, bike racks
Description:	Slightly rolling, with the grass nearly all parched. Small areas of shade. Paved path running across the front and down one side. Fenced except on street side. Some traffic noise from Benton. Indoor sports center.
Of Note:	If you really wanted a workout, you could walk between Homestead and Central parks (there are sidewalks all the way) and explore both.

Walk 10: Steve Carli Park

Location:	Los Padres Blvd. off Benton Street—easy to find. See Map 14.
Size:	3 acres, about two-thirds open grass
Parking:	Neighborhood street parking
For Comfort:	Restrooms (locked); water fountain
For Sports:	Basketball court, 2 softball fields, one fenced and locked, with covered bleachers
For Kids:	2 playgrounds

Description:	Flat ground, with nice grass. Some limited shade. Some resident squirrels. Large paved area around first playground, otherwise no path of any kind.
Of Note:	If you have a dog that likes balls, there's a chance of finding some Little League softballs lost in the grass.

Walk 11: Fremont Park

Location:	Fremont Street off Lincoln Blvd.—easy to find. See Map 14.
Size:	7 acres, all open grass
Parking:	Neighborhood street parking, or lot at adjacent Senior Center
For Comfort:	Water fountain
For Sports:	Parcourse, horseshoe pits
For Kids:	Playground
Description:	Nearly flat ground, with nice grass. Some limited shade. Paved lighted path running across and through, with benches spaced along it. Quiet.
Of Note:	The park is adjacent to the Santa Clara County Senior Citizen Center, and there is a memorial rose garden tucked in at one side of the center, which is a real treat in the spring.

Walk 12: Lafayette Park

Location:	Lewis Street and Lafayette Street—easy to locate but something of a challenge to get to, due to one-way streets. See Map 14.
Size:	5 acres, nearly all softball field
Parking:	Large lot off Lafayette
For Comfort:	Restrooms (locked unless the fields are reserved for play); water fountain

For Sports: Lighted softball field with bleachers

Description: Flat, with good grass, and absolutely no shade. Completely fenced.

Of Note: Although, unlike the playing fields at Washington Park, dogs are permitted here, there really isn't much aside from the softball field. Still, you may find a stray ball lying about to play with.

Walk 13: Warburton Park

Location: Los Padres Drive off El Camino Real—easy to find. See Map 14.

Size: 6 acres, about half open grass

Parking: Lot with 30 spaces off Royal Drive

For Comfort: Restrooms with Swim Center (locked when pool is closed); water fountain

For Sports: Swimming pool, basketball court

For Dining: 11 picnic tables, 3 barbecues

For Kids: Playground

Description: Flat, with patchy grass. Shade is mostly around edge of park along back-yard fences. Paved path around pool. Fenced on two sides. Reasonably quiet.

Of Note: As the sign says, this is the Warburton Swim Center, and that's mostly what the park is dedicated to, although there are other facilities.

Walk 14: Bowers Park

Location: Cabrillo Avenue—easy to find. See Map 14.

Size: 7 acres, mostly open grass

Parking: Neighborhood street parking; what was once a parking lot is now blocked off

For Comfort: Restrooms (locked); water fountain

For Sports: 5 game tables under shade arbors

For Dining: 15 picnic tables, 7 barbecues

For Kids: Playground, bike racks

Description: Nearly flat, with grass being parched by the drought. Areas of shade under trees and arbors. Paved, lighted path across length of park to Barkley Avenue at the other end. A currently dry canal runs along one side. There is a building with two rooms that appear to be set up for lectures, separated by a shade arbor. There is also an odd lighted concrete circle, with no apparent use. Some trees appear to be dying.

Of Note: This is a good-sized park without any sports facilities, where you can just walk or sit in the shade.

Walk 15: Machado Park

Location: Cabrillo Avenue—easy to find. See Map 14.

Size: 3.5 acres, about three-quarters open grass

Parking: Neighborhood street parking

For Comfort: Restrooms (locked); water fountain

For Sports: Basketball court, softball field with bleachers

For Dining: 5 picnic tables, 5 barbecues

For Kids: Playground

Description: Mostly small rolling hills, with mediocre grass. Nice patches of shade. Lighted, paved path across front. Backs onto school yard. Quiet.

Of Note: There is a noisy dog in an adjacent back yard, who can almost make it over the top of his fence.

Walk 16: Bracher Park

Location: Cortez Drive off Chromlte Drive off Bowers Avenue—a little hard to find. See Map 14.

Size: 3.5 acres, nearly all open grass

Parking: Neighborhood street parking

For Comfort: Restrooms (locked); water fountain not functioning

For Sports: Basketball court

For Dining: 3 picnic tables, 3 small tables where barbecues used to be

For Kids: Playground, bike racks

Description: Flat center rolls up to higher ground around the edges. Grass dying in places from the drought. Fenced except for the street side. Railroad runs directly behind. Good areas of shade. Paved path around perimeter, with a pedestrian walkway over Bowers. Some traffic noise.

Of Note: Santa Clara's parks are neat and clean, but this one is a prime example of how such facilities as restrooms and water fountains seem to be low on the city's list of priorities.

Walk 17: Montague Park

Location: De La Cruz Blvd. south of Montague Expwy.—easy to find. See Map 14.

Size: 5.5 acres, about three-quarters open grass

Parking: Neighborhood street parking

For Comfort: Restrooms (locked); water fountain

For Sports: 2 tennis courts, basketball court

For Dining: 4 picnic tables, 2 barbecues

For Kids: 2 playgrounds

Description: Mostly rolling, with grass areas in the sun. Groupings of trees with areas of deep shade under them. Paved, lighted path running across length in curve. Powerlines down one side of park. Quiet, except for plane noise overhead.

Of Note: This park has a good mix of sun and especially intense shade. There are also several types of playground equipment in the different areas.

Walk 18: Agnew Park

Location: Agnew Road off Lafayette Street—easy to find. See
                   Map 14.

Size: 2 acres, about three-quarters open grass

Parking: Neighborhood street parking

For Comfort: Restrooms (locked); water fountain

For Sports: Basketball court

For Dining: 7 picnic tables

For Kids: Playground

Description: Flat in the center with small hills all around. Good
                   grass. Lots of nice shade areas. Fenced on all but the
                   street side. Paved lighted path around perimeter. Lots
                   of benches, and a small open amphitheater. An uni-
                   dentified locked building sits in the center of the park.

Of Note: There is more landscaping than in most parks, making
                   for a very attractive, though small, park.

Walk 19: Fairway Glen Park

Location: Calle de Primavera off Lafayette Street—easy to find.
                   See Map 14.

Size: 5 acres, nearly all open grass

Parking: Neighborhood street parking

For Comfort: Water fountain

For Sports: 2 tennis courts

For Dining: 2 picnic tables, 2 barbecues

For Kids: Playground

Description: Definitely rolling, with lush grass. Nice patches of
                   shade from groupings of small trees. Paved path wind-
                   ing across to adjacent school yard. Unfenced. Some
                   landscaping. Occasional plane noise overhead.

Of Note: This is the farthest north of Santa Clara's parks, and
                   the only one in its area.

Chapter 3
Campbell

As stated in the chapter introduction, Campbell is the only community in Santa Clara County to maintain a no-dogs-allowed policy in its parks. Since there are only two city parks within Campbell, the impact is not large in area, but if you happen to live in Campbell, and pay your taxes, there's a definite feeling of being discriminated against. San Jose pretty nearly surrounds Campbell, so parks are available, but having to leave town to visit a park, even if it's only a mile down the road, is not a pleasant feeling. However, Campbell does have the following two dog-walking places.

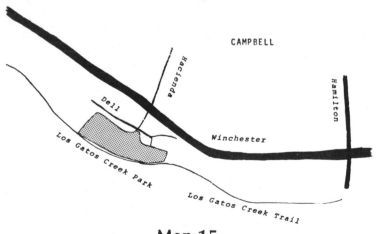

Map 15

Walk 1: Los Gatos Creek Park

Location: Entry from Dell Avenue—a little hard to find. See Map 15.

Size: County gave no size; perhaps 20 acres.

Parking: 2 lots, sometimes with a fee

For Comfort: Restrooms, clean; water fountains

For Sports: Fishing, windsurfing

For Dining: Picnic tables, barbecues

Description: A large, mostly flat field with a few small trees. Not much shade. Fenced along one side, bordered by water on much of the other three sides. Receives quite a lot of use. Broken glass and litter can be a problem at times. The Los Gatos Creek Trail runs through at one side.

Of Note: A dog show is held here about once a month, with both conformation and obedience to watch.

Walk 2: Los Gatos Creek Trail

Location: Runs along Campbell Park and Los Gatos Creek Park. See Map 15.

Size: Approximately 3 linear miles

Parking: Most accessible in Los Gatos Creek Park, or you can find a space on the side streets around Campbell Park

For Comfort: Restrooms and water fountain in Los Gatos Creek Park

For Sports: Parcourse in Campbell Park (but dogs not allowed)

For Dining: Picnic tables and barbecues in Los Gatos Creek Park

Description: Mostly flat paved path along Los Gatos Creek. Runs from Hamilton Avenue, where Campbell meets San Jose, to the end of the Camden Percolation Ponds, where Campbell meets Los Gatos, and continues on through Los Gatos to Lexington Reservoir Dam. Mostly in the sun, but a few patches of shade. There are restrooms, water fountains and picnic tables in Los Gatos Creek Park, if you care to take a break from your walk or jog.

Chapter 4
Los Gatos

Los Gatos is rather small and indeed still calls itself a town rather than a city. It has eight parks within its boundaries, and most of them are real standouts. The usual leash and clean-up laws apply.

You can really do some walking in Los Gatos parks. There are fine, civilized, paved-path outings in Vasona and La Rinconada. There are about 4 miles of good trail along Los Gatos Creek, shared with joggers and bicyclists. And there's hill climbing in Belgatos and Novitiate. Of course there are the more usual city parks as well. Even a walk downtown is enjoyable.

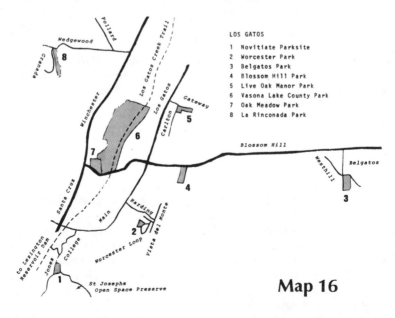

LOS GATOS

1 Novitiate Parksite
2 Worcester Park
3 Belgatos Park
4 Blossom Hill Park
5 Live Oak Manor Park
6 Vasona Lake County Park
7 Oak Meadow Park
8 La Rinconada Park

Map 16

Walk 1: Novitiate Park

Location: End of Jones Road off College Avenue off East Main Street—kind of hard to find. See Map 16.

Size: 8 acres, all open space

Parking: Limited neighborhood street parking

Description: Los Gatos has not yet developed this park, and it consists of a large open meadow on a hillside, with a dirt trail running across it. It would not be notable at all, except that the trail leads to St. Josephs Open Space Preserve, and a lovely long, shady, strenuous trail where dogs are allowed on leash. Plenty of local joggers and bicyclists use the trail, although there is a section where all are required to walk due to the steepness of the trail.

Of Note: There are, of course, the usual ticks you encounter when you get into real open space. But the trail through St. Josephs is long and pleasant, if a bit steep at times. If you time your visit right, you can even have a taste of wine just down the road at the Novitiate Winery.

Walk 2: Worcester Park

Location: Worcester Loop off Worcester Lane—hard to find. See Map 16.

Size: 11.2 acres, all natural

Parking: Neighborhood street parking

Description: This is very much a park on a hill. Paved paths wind up and down, with a total length of maybe 0.3 mile. There are numbered markers, obviously meant to identify plants, but there were no brochures in the information box on my visit. There are benches for those who need to rest after a climb, or just want to sit and contemplate. The paths wind in and out of sun and shade. There is poison oak in the park, so know what it looks like before you go. You can end up itching not only if you touch it, but also if your dog rubs through it and you then pet your dog.

Of Note: The park itself is quite clean, but the sidewalk and gutter running along the front is littered with dog droppings.

Walk 3: Belgatos Park

Location: Belgatos Road off Blossom Hill Road—a bit hard to find. See Map 16.

Size: 17 acres, perhaps an acre in grass, the rest natural

Parking: Lot partly hidden at end of Belgatos

For Comfort: Restrooms, with wheelchair access, reasonably clean; water fountain

For Sports: Trails are used by bicyclists and equestrians

For Dining: Picnic tables set in woods amid trees, and group picnic area on far side of creek

For Kids: Playground

Description: This is a park with a small tamed area containing the playground, restrooms, and a grass area. The rest of the park is natural, with small suspension bridges across the creek and dirt trails leading over the hills. The gain in elevation on most trails is enough to increase your heart rate. Shorter paths in loops are lighted, main path over hill is not. Main path comes out on Harwood Drive, about 1 mile away.

Of Note: You can really get a workout climbing these hills, and dogs seem to find it fascinating. But there are a lot of ticks, so take precautions.

Walk 4: Blossom Hill Park

Location: Blossom Hill Road at one end, Shannon Road at the other—easy to find. See Map 16.

Size: 9.2 acres, nearly all open grass

Parking: Small lot on Blossom Hill, larger lot on Shannon

For Comfort: Water fountains

For Sports: 6 lighted tennis courts, parcourse

For Kids: Playground

Description: Small rolling hills, with very nice grass. Some well-done landscaping. Good areas of shade. Paved path across length, with benches scattered along it. Very peaceful at the Shannon side, some traffic noise at the Blossom Hill side. Seems to be well used by tennis enthusiasts and dog owners.

Of Note: This is a very attractive city park, somewhat more pleasant in the half toward Shannon because of reduced traffic noise.

Walk 5: Live Oak Manor Park

Location: Gateway Drive off Los Gatos Blvd.—easy to find. See Map 16.

Size: 4.1 acres, nearly all open grass

Parking: Neighborhood street parking

For Comfort: Water fountain

For Sports: Basketball court

For Kids: Playground

Description: Mostly flat, with a few tiny hills for variety. Nice grass, with pleasant patches of shade, but not a lot of it. Lighted dirt path, with benches spaced along it, runs length of park. High powerlines run above the park. Fenced along neighbors' back yards down length. Quiet.

Of Note: This is a smallish park without any real distinguishing features, but it does have a pleasant air about it, and is easy to get to.

Walk 6: Vasona Lake County Park

Location: Blossom Hill Road at University Avenue—easy to find. See Map 16.

Size: 151 acres

Parking: Several lots scattered through the park

For Comfort: Restrooms in several areas, with wheelchair access, clean; water fountains throughout the park

For Sports: Boating (rentals in the summer)

For Dining: Several group picnic areas, with barbecues

For Kids: Playground

Description: Large park containing a reservoir and a small stream, both called home by a variety of ducks, geese, coots and gulls. Slightly rolling terrain with nice grass. Good areas of shade. Some traffic noise from 17, otherwise quiet. Paved path around the reservoir. The park connects with Oak Meadow Park. Well used by joggers and bicyclists.

Of Note: In summer, there is a fee. In winter, the gate is not manned. County regulations regarding dogs are not always clear. Here, the only sign indicates dogs must be on a leash. The county handout I received indicates that dogs are allowed only from 8 to 10 A.M. and 4 to 5 P.M. However, the rangers with whom I spoke were not aware of this restriction. In the winter, there is unlikely to be any problem. In the summer, when the park is crowded, you may not be allowed in during midday.

Walk 7: Oak Meadow Park

Location: Blossom Hill Road at University Avenue—easy to find. See Map 16.

Size: 12 acres, about two-thirds open space, some grass, some natural

Parking: Large lot off Blossom Hill

For Comfort: Restrooms with wheelchair access, clean; water fountains

For Dining: Several group picnic areas

For Kids: Miniature railroad to ride through Oak Meadow and Vasona (open Easter to Labor Day); old plane to climb on; playground; carrousel.

Description: Grass area flat, natural hillside with picnic area at one side. Plenty of shade. Paved path around. Quiet. Connects with Vasona Lake County Park. Creek forms boundary between parks.

Of Note: This is a very popular park, and for good reason. The kids will love the park, but dogs are *not* allowed on the train.

Walk 8: La Rinconada Park

Location: Granada Way off Wedgewood Avenue—a little hard to find. See Map 16.

Size: 14 acres, nearly all open space, some in parklike grass, some left natural

Parking: Neighborhood street parking

For Comfort: Water fountain

For Sports: 1 tennis court, parcourse

For Dining: 9 picnic tables, 4 barbecues

For Kids: Playground

Description: Mostly flat park, with tamed section long and narrow, paved path leading off into the woods. Pleasant live creek along back of tamed section, with bridges across for path. Mostly shaded. Some picnic tables in tamed section, some along path in woods. Parcourse starts in grass, follows path through woods, and ends in grass. Path about ½ mile long.

Of Note: This is a very pretty park, with the bonus of offering visitors a highly civilized walk through the woods without much fear of ticks and fleas.

Walk 9: St. Josephs Open-Space Preserve

Location: Between Los Gatos and Lexington Reservoir—trail-heads on Alma Bridge Road at Lexington Reservoir and Jones Road in Los Gatos. See Map 16.

Size: 170 acres, all natural with trails

Parking: Street parking on Jones Road, lot east of Lexington Reservoir dam

Description: A hill and valley left in their natural state and very much a wildlife refuge. Happily for us, dogs are allowed on leash. From Jones Road, the trail goes up gradually for about 1/10 mile, then climbs steeply for 3/10 with joggers and bicyclists requested to walk. The trail winds from sun to shade, and can be muddy in the shade even after very little precipitation. At the start, Route 17 is not far away, and there is plenty of traffic noise, but after the steep uphill climb, the trail moves away from the road and becomes quieter. There are beautiful twisted madrones in a small meadow in a flat section, then the trail heads off up, then down, St. Josephs Hill, to end approximately 4 miles away at Alma Bridge Road.

Of Note:	If you want more of a workout than a city park affords, this is the place for you. If you're lucky enough to have someone to bring a car around, you can start at Alma Bridge Road and have most of your work done at the beginning of the hike.

Walk 10: Los Gatos Creek Trail

Location:	Along Los Gatos Creek from Campbell border to Lexington Reservoir—best access in Vasona County Park. See Map 16.
Size:	55 acres, all natural with dirt or paved trail
Parking:	Various lots in Vasona, or street locations in Los Gatos
Description:	Ultimately, this path is supposed to connect Lexington Reservoir with the Guadalupe corridor in downtown San Jose. For now, it runs completely through Campbell and Los Gatos and on up to Lexington. Within Los Gatos, it amounts to approximately 4 miles of trail. From the Campbell border through Vasona County Park, the trail is mostly flat and sometimes paved. After that it starts to climb, gradually at first, more steeply as you near the reservoir. Some stretches of the path are shaded, but most are in the sun. There are sections where the creek is easily accessible and your dog can cool his feet and have a drink. On any given day you will share the path with joggers and bicyclists.

Walk 11: A Miscellaneous Walk Downtown Los Gatos

Location:	Santa Cruz Avenue, Main Street, Los Gatos Blvd. See Map 16.
Parking:	Various streets and lots downtown

Description: Los Gatos is often described in guidebooks as a charming Mediterranean-style town. Unfortunately, some of its older buildings tumbled in the Loma Prieta earthquake, but Los Gatos remains a vibrant, special town. The sidewalks are wide and the shops have awnings, and there are plenty of shops.

If you like to window-shop, and your dog is well-behaved amid crowds, this could be your perfect outing. There are antique shops, book stores, brass shops, specialty stores. If you want to do some real shopping, come with a friend and take turns holding each other's dogs.

Chapter 5
Saratoga

Saratoga, a small community, does not have a large number of parks. But those it has are interesting and attractive. Hidden pathways lead out of several and wind behind back-yard fences to other roads. Or you can walk along the railroad tracks that run through town and past several of the parks. The nicest park, Wildwood, requires a walk to get to, since there is no parking at the park, but rewards you with a charming stream.

There are, of course, a leash law and a clean-up ordinance. Saratoga's largest green areas, Villa Montalvo and Hakone Gardens, are closed to dogs. Visit them sometime without your canine companion.

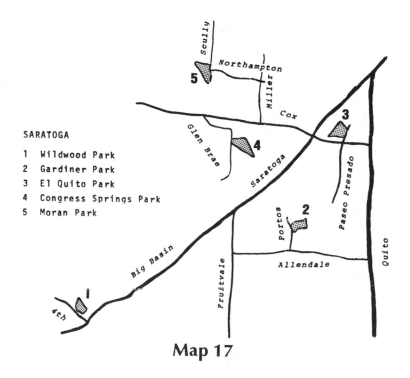

SARATOGA

1 Wildwood Park
2 Gardiner Park
3 El Quito Park
4 Congress Springs Park
5 Moran Park

Map 17

Walk 1: Wildwood Park

Location: 4th Street off Big Basin Way—easy to find. See Map 17.

Size: 4 acres, nearly all open, with about an acre of grass and the rest natural

Parking: Very limited street parking, and lot meant for the Saratoga Inn

For Comfort: Restrooms, reasonably clean; water fountain

For Sports: Sand volleyball court, horseshoe pit

For Dining: 5 picnic tables, 5 barbecues; 2 small group areas, with 5 tables and 1 large barbecue each

For Kids: Playground, bike racks

Description: Hillside leading down to a very attractive live creek. Some grass but mostly natural. Lots of shade. Wide paved path leading through.

Of Note: Parking is terrible. It might be wiser to park in one of the city lots and walk down 4th to the park. The creek is very accessible and enjoyable.

Walk 2: Gardiner Park

Location: Portos Drive off Allendale Avenue—hard to find. See Map 17.

Size: 2.2 acres, nearly all open space

Parking: Neighborhood street parking

For Dining: 1 picnic table

For Kids: Playground

Description: Tiny hills, with somewhat sparse grass. Good shade trees. Paved path through park. Fenced along sides, not ends. Quiet other than dogs barking in back yards facing the park.

Of Note: The park is small, but a dirt path continues from the end of the park behind back-yard fences along creek to

Riverdale Drive off Aspesi Drive. Across Portos a less defined dirt path also winds between back-yard fences and the creek to a court off Harleigh Drive. The paths probably cover a total distance of about ½ mile.

Walk 3: El Quito Park

Location: Paseo Presado off Cox Avenue—easy to find. See Map 17.

Size: 6.3 acres, about three-quarters open grass

Parking: Neighborhood street parking

For Comfort: Restrooms with wheelchair access, extremely clean in attractive building; water fountains, including fountains accessible to dogs

For Sports: Softball field with bleachers, soccer field, parcourse, horseshoe pits, 2 chess tables

For Dining: 2 picnic tables, 2 barbecues; group area of 3 picnic tables with large barbecue

For Kids: Playground, bike racks

Description: Mostly flat, with good grass. Paved path runs almost completely around. Some limited shade. Mostly fenced. Quiet. Next to community garden at one end.

Of Note: A "relaxation" parcourse, different than most, runs along two sides of the park, making a pleasantly invigorating workout that you can manage with your dog.

Walk 4: Congress Springs Park

Location: Glenbrae Drive off Cox Avenue—easy to find. See Map 17.

Size: 19.7 acres, mostly softball fields

Parking: Lot off Glenbrae

For Comfort: Restrooms with wheelchair access, extremely clean; water fountains, one accessible to dogs

For Sports: 4 softball fields with bleachers

For Kids: Playground, bike racks

Description: Flat, with most of the area taken up by the playing fields. Dogs are allowed on the fields when games are not in progress. No shade. Fields are fenced. One side runs along railroad tracks.

Of Note: If you like walking along the railroad tracks, which seems to be popular in this area, the park is a good place to stop and get a drink or use the restrooms.

Walk 5: Moran Park

Location: Scully Avenue off Prospect Road—easy to find. See Map 17.

Size: 10.3 acres, nearly all open grass or orchard

Parking: Neighborhood street parking

For Comfort: Water fountain, accessible to dogs

For Dining: 3 picnic tables

For Kids: Playground, bike racks

Description: Slightly sloping, with lush grass in large middle area, old orchards at both ends. Paved path with scattered benches loops around park. Good areas of both sun and shade. Unfenced. Quiet.

Of Note: A large attractive park with a good walk around the perimeter. In such an exclusive neighborhood, it's surprising to hear chickens from a house nearby.

Chapter 6
Cupertino

Cupertino offers a fine variety of open areas, with eleven city parks, one county park, and an open space preserve. Dogs are allowed in all but one of the city parks, but there are additional restrictions in the county park. Otherwise there's the usual duo of leash and clean-up laws.

Of the city parks, Linda Vista is the crown jewel. There, you can have an exhilarating climb or a cooling walk by a waterfall. Memorial Park is also large and water-oriented, being made even larger as this book is being written. Here families of ducks and geese offer great entertainment for most canine visitors.

Walk 1: Hoover Park

Location:	Leeds Avenue—a little hard to find. See Map 18.
Size:	5 acres, all open grass
Parking:	2 small lots on Leeds
For Comfort:	Water fountain
For Sports:	2 soccer fields, basketball court
For Kids:	2 playground areas
Description:	Flat L-shaped park with weedy grass. No shade except at one end. Paved path only to the first playground. Quiet.
Of Note:	This is a fairly new park. It will certainly be prettier when the new trees have had a chance to grow and the grass to become a bit more like a lawn. There may be other facilities added as the park is completed.

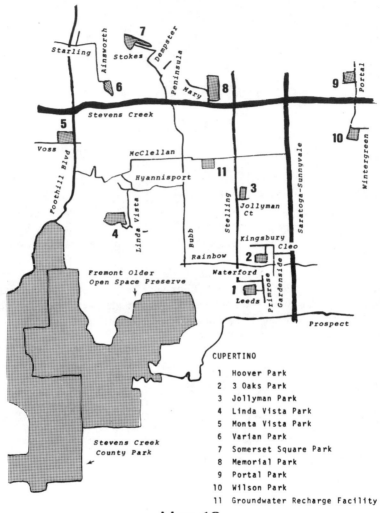

CUPERTINO

1 Hoover Park
2 3 Oaks Park
3 Jollyman Park
4 Linda Vista Park
5 Monta Vista Park
6 Varian Park
7 Somerset Square Park
8 Memorial Park
9 Portal Park
10 Wilson Park
11 Groundwater Recharge Facility

Map 18

Walk 2: 3 Oaks Park

Location: Shadowhill Lane off Stelling Road—easy to find. See Map 18.

Size: 3.1 acres, all open grass

Parking: Small lot off Shadowhill or street parking

For Comfort:	Water fountain
For Dining:	6 picnic tables, 6 barbecues
For Kids:	2 playgrounds

Description: Slightly rolling with grass just starting to parch. Shade areas under two large oaks (maybe the third died?). Lighted, paved path winding through length. Unfenced. Quiet.

Of Note: One playground has a sort of mini-Stonehenge, with rock bridges across sand. The large oaks and general layout of the park are very attractive.

Walk 3: Jollyman Park

Location: Jollyman Court off Stelling Road—easy to find. See Map 18.

Size: 11.5 acres is the size given by Cupertino Parks, but it doesn't look anywhere near that; more like 5 acres, but it's all open

Parking: Small lot at end of Jollyman Court

For Comfort: Water fountain

For Sports: Soccer field, baseball field

For Dining: 2 picnic tables

For Kids: Playground

Description: Mostly flat with good grass. Nice shade areas. Paved path across width. Mostly fenced. Quiet. Evidence of use by mountain bikers.

Of Note: Although apparently not as large as advertised, this park does seem to be little used, and might be a nice place to bring a dog that doesn't do well with crowds. If you do come, be sure to visit the water fountain, possibly the only interior-landscaped fountain I've ever seen.

Walk 4: Linda Vista Park

Location:	Linda Vista Drive—easy to find. See Map 18.
Size:	11 acres, all open, mostly natural
Parking:	Large lot off Linda Vista Drive
For Comfort:	Restrooms, basic but clean and wheelchair-accessible; water fountains
For Sports:	Fitness station; playing field
For Dining:	Group area for 100 people; 4 individual tables partway up hill; 5 individual tables and 2 barbecues down by water area
For Kids:	2 playgrounds
Description:	This is mostly a large hill left in a fairly natural state, with a flat playing field and a pond at the bottom. In wetter times, there is a waterfall. On my visit, there was only a pond. Paved path goes perhaps a third of the way up the hill, then loops down to the water. A dirt path continues on up. Park abuts Deep Cliff golf course.
Of Note:	This is a gorgeous park. If you really want a workout, take the rough, narrow dirt path up to the top of the hill. An easier trip is down the paved path to the water area, where dogs can wade.

Walk 5: Monta Vista Park

Location:	Voss Avenue off Foothill Blvd.—easy to find. See Map 18.
Size:	6.2 acres, about two-thirds open
Parking:	Large lot off Voss
For Comfort:	Restrooms (locked on my visit); water fountains
For Sports:	2 tennis courts, softball field, recreation center for rhythmic gymnastics and other indoor sports
For Dining:	5 picnic tables, 5 barbecues

For Kids:	2 playgrounds
Description:	Flat with some small mounds. Limited shade. Paved path around the recreation buildings. Lighted generally. Softball field is fenced. Some traffic noise.
Of Note:	This is more a sportsman's park than a dog owner's, but there are large patches of green around the buildings and tennis courts.

Walk 6: Varian Park

Location:	Varian Way off Ainsworth Drive—hard to find. See Map 18.
Size:	6.3 acres, nearly all open
Parking:	Lot off Varian Way
For Comfort:	Water fountain
For Sports:	2 tennis courts
For Dining:	6 picnic tables, 6 barbecues
For Kids:	2 playgrounds
Description:	Mostly flat, grassy area amid the trees of an old orchard. Not much shade, because the trees are small, as fruit trees should be. Mostly fenced. Paved, lighted path around perimeter. Quiet.
Of Note:	If you find this one on the map, you'll see no obvious way in, and it took quite a bit of driving to find the entrance. Still, now that you know which road to take, this is a very lovely park in the springtime when the orchard is in bloom.

Walk 7: Somerset Square Park

Location:	Stokes Avenue a little hard to find. See Map 18.
Size:	1.7 acres, nearly all open grass
Parking:	Small lot at end of Stokes Avenue
For Comfort:	Water fountain

For Sports: Basketball court, volleyball court (no net)

For Dining: 3 picnic tables, 2 barbecues

For Kids: Playground

Description: Mostly flat, with some tiny hills. Good lush grass. Lots of shade, which is probably why the grass is still unparched. Paved path around perimeter of main part of park, with a weedy area extending off one end under high powerlines. Mostly fenced. Lots of traffic noise from 280.

Of Note: If you like to sit and watch traffic go by, this is the park for you. There's a bench on a knoll directly overlooking 280.

Walk 8: Memorial Park

Location: Stevens Creek Blvd. and Mary Avenue—easy to find. See Map 18.

Size: Approximately 20 acres

Parking: Lot off Mary

For Comfort: Restrooms with wheelchair access, very clean; water fountains

For Sports: 6 lighted tennis courts, lighted softball field with bleachers

For Dining: 10 picnic tables and 9 barbecues on Stevens Creek side; large group area and 6 individual tables and 4 barbecues at one side of rear; 3 tables at other side of rear

For Kids: Playground with Western false-front miniature buildings in front; small playground in back

Description: Hilly, with nice grass areas. Very active duck ponds, with ducks, geese and gulls. Amphitheater set into hillside. Shaded gazebo with benches across bridge in middle of pond. Other shade limited. Busy senior/community center at front. Ponds are kept wet for the ducks and geese, but the stream that usually flows through is dry during the drought.

Of Note:	The park is in the process of being expanded, with more sports and community facilities to come. The tennis courts and group picnic area are new additions.

Walk 9: Portal Park

Location:	Portal Avenue off Stevens Creek Blvd.—easy to find. See Map 18.
Size:	3.8 acres, nearly all open
Parking:	Neighborhood street parking
For Comfort:	Restrooms, with wheelchair access, clean; water fountain
For Dining:	Group area for 60; 4 individual picnic tables, 2 barbecues
For Kids:	Large playground with castlelike structures, turrets and "cannons"
Description:	Small hills rolling one into another. Slightly weedy grass. Good areas of shade. Paved path winding through length. Community building currently used by a preschool. Quiet.
Of Note:	Some of the preschoolers were not very good around dogs, trying to poke mine with sticks and screaming and running away. But the preschool hopes to be moving soon, so this shouldn't be a problem.

Walk 10: Wilson Park

Location:	Wintergreen Drive off Portal Avenue—easy to find. See Map 18.
Size:	4.8 acres, all open
Parking:	Neighborhood street parking
For Comfort:	Restrooms with wheelchair access, clean; water fountain
For Sports:	Fitness course; softball and soccer fields at adjacent school

For Dining: 6 picnic tables, 4 barbecues

For Kids: 3 playground areas

Description: Sloping ground with small hills. Grass is okay. Paved lighted path leading around perimeter to fitness stations. Some shade areas, and some landscaping. Quiet. Community building.

Of Note: The playgrounds and fitness stations scattered all over the park are mostly constructed from large logs in various configurations, and add a lot of visual interest to the park.

Walk 11: Groundwater Recharge Facility

Location: Bubb Road near McClellan Road—easy to find. See Map 18.

Description: This is not a Cupertino park—it is one of the many areas owned by Santa Clara County Water District. But this is certainly one of the most attractive groundwater recharge facilities in the county. The pond is fenced, and there is landscaping all the way around, with a pleasant path and benches for relaxing. There is no shade to speak of, and parking could be a problem. But if you want somewhere to sit and have lunch and watch some water, and Memorial Park is just too crowded, this may be the place.

Walk 12: Stevens Creek County Park

Location: Stevens Canyon Road—easy to find. See Map 18.

Size: Approximately 1,000 acres

Parking: Various lots along the road or side road

For Comfort: Some picnic areas have regular restrooms, some have portable toilets; some picnic areas have water fountains

For Sports: Archery range; horseshoe pits in Villa Maria picnic area

For Dining: Various areas

Description: Hilly park left mostly in its natural state. Stevens Canyon and Mt. Eden roads lead through. Deer, coyote and perhaps even a mountain lion live here. So do poison oak, rattlesnakes and other things to avoid. We once met an injured bat who couldn't fly, but was still intent on defending himself.

Of Note: Dogs are allowed only in picnic areas that are not signed against them. As you enter the park take a left down to the ranger station. There are three areas there where dogs are permitted, the nicest being at the top of the hill at Villa Maria. Let your dog lead you around and watch for tracks and other signs of last night's wildlife.

Walk 13: Fremont Older Open-Space Preserve

Location: End of Prospect Road—a little hard to find. See Map 18.

Size: 734 acres, all open with trails except small area around Fremont Older home

Parking: Small lot at end of road

Description: A hilly, mostly natural area, frequented by coyote and deer. Gravel road leads past the former home of news-paperman Fremont Older. Trail leads through small stand of forest. Beyond that, most trails are in the sun until you are well on your way toward Stevens Creek County Park. All trails climb up and down, and there are few flat areas. Dogs are not allowed on trails in Stevens Creek Park, so when you reach the boundary you have to turn back. Trails total 4.5 miles.

Of Note: This is a fine hiking park as long as it's not too hot. If you come early or late, you may see some wildlife. Be aware that the park is also home to poison oak and rattlesnakes. Don't let your dog poke his nose under rocks or into holes.

Walk 14: A Miscellaneous Walk
De Anza College

Location: Stevens Creek Blvd. at Mary Avenue—easy to find. See Map 18.

Size: Approximately 50 acres

Parking: Various lots on two sides of the campus

For Comfort: Water fountains and restrooms in some buildings

For Sports: Archery range, track, swimming pool

Description: Nicely landscaped campus, with some areas of shade but mostly sun. Paths mostly run between buildings. One corner is a study garden for endangered plants. Recycling center is at back.

Of Note: Dog shows are sometimes held on the multi-use field, and the Humane Society's "Care-a-Thon," including an 8K walk with your dog, is held here.

Chapter 7
Sunnyvale

Sunnyvale has probably the most thoroughly landscaped and manicured parks in Santa Clara County. They contain lots of free-standing walls and shade arbors breaking space up into smaller, more secluded areas. Several have sizable pavilions that would serve well for outdoor group functions. These, and the small buildings found in most Sunnyvale parks, can be reserved through the Community Center (408/730-7500). Most of the picnic areas are set up for groups, but are available to everyone as long as they're not reserved. Remember the leash and pooper-scooper laws.

If you want a walk on the wild side, head out to the Baylands. The county areas, which compose the majority of the Baylands, are open to dogs. You can bushwhack across country or use the levee system of Santa Clara Water District, and really walk. There are egrets in abundance, and other waterfowl.

Walk 1: Raynor Park

Location: Quail Avenue off Homestead Road—easy to find. See Map 19.

Size: 7 acres, nearly all open grass

Parking: Large lot off Quail

For Comfort: Restrooms with wheelchair access, clean; water fountains

For Sports: Horseshoe pits, softball field with bleachers

For Dining: 3 group areas; 3 individual picnic tables, 2 barbecues

SUNNYVALE

1   Raynor Park
2   Panama Park
3   Ortega Park
4   Serra Park
5   San Antonio Park
6   De Anza Park
7   Las Palmas Park
8   Braly Park
9   Ponderosa Park
10 Washington Park
11 Murphy Historical Park
12 Fair Oaks Park
13 Orchard Gardens Park
14 Lakewood Park
15 Fairwood Park

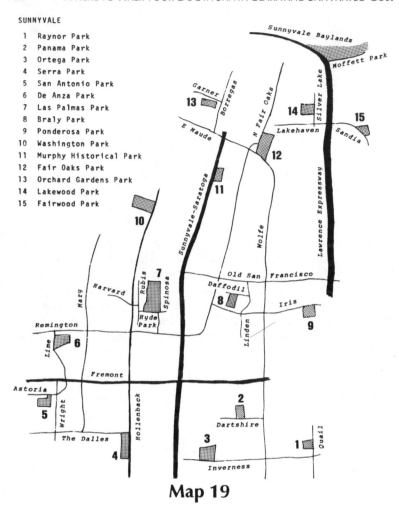

Map 19

For Kids: Playground with dinosaurs to climb on

Description: Mostly flat, with lush grass. Lighted, paved path run-
                     ning across park in two places and to adjacent school.
                     Several nice areas of shade. Lots of landscaping, and
                     plenty of birds singing. Quiet. Two-room building
                     available for reservation through the Sunnyvale Com-
                     munity Center.

Of Note: This is a good-sized park with an odd corner or two for
                     some privacy.

Walk 2: Panama Park

Location:	Dartshire Way off Wolfe Road—easy to find. See Map 19.
Size:	4.91 acres, all open grass
Parking:	Lot off Dartshire
For Comfort:	Restrooms with wheelchair access, clean; water fountain
For Sports:	Softball field with bleachers, soccer field
Description:	Flat, open field with very little shade. Path leads only around the restrooms. Completely fenced.
Of Note:	This is really just a ball field.

Walk 3: Ortega Park

Location:	Inverness Way off Wolfe Road—easy to find. See Map 19.
Size:	15 acres, about three-quarters open grass
Parking:	Large and small lots off Harrow Way
For Comfort:	Restrooms with wheelchair access, clean; water fountains; pay phone
For Sports:	2 lighted tennis courts, lighted basketball courts, lighted softball field with bleachers, shuffleboard, horseshoe pits, 4 game tables
For Dining:	Group areas for 75 people at each end of park
For Kids:	Large multi-area playground; bike racks
Description:	Mostly gently rolling, broken into large lawns and smaller, more secluded areas by various shade arbors, plantings and free-standing walls. Plenty of both sun and shade areas. Lighted, paved path looping through length and width. Lush grass. Lots of landscaping. Lovely mature trees. Large covered pavilion and community building.

Of Note: This looks like the perfect place for a wedding reception, with a brick path leading up to the pavilion across a wide green lawn. It's certainly an appealing park, even if you're just walking your dog.

Walk 4: Serra Park

Location: Hollenbeck Avenue at The Dalles—easy to find. See Map 19.

Size: 8.5 acres originally, plus 4.65-acre addition; about two-thirds open grass

Parking: Large lot off Hollenbeck

For Comfort: Restrooms with wheelchair access, clean; water fountains; pay phone

For Sports: 4 lighted tennis courts, shuffleboard, softball field

For Dining: 4 group areas, to seat 40, 20, 50 and 90

For Kids: 2 playground areas, one conventional, one a mockup of a riverboat

Description: Slightly rolling terrain, good grass. Lots of shade areas. Lighted, paved path winding around perimeter of park. Good blend of open lawn and trees/landscaped areas. Small pavilion area and community building. Some traffic noise from Hollenbeck. Heavily used.

Of Note: In wetter times, there is a stream running all through the park and into a small pond, but this has been drained during the drought.

Walk 5: San Antonio Park

Location: Astoria Drive off Wright Avenue—a little hard to find. See Map 19.

Size: 6 acres, mostly open grass

Parking: School lot on Astoria or neighborhood street parking

For Sports: Softball field, 2 soccer fields, basketball courts, volleyball court

For Kids: Playground at adjacent school

Description: Flat, open field with very limited shade around the edges. Paved path leads only a short way into an arm of the park. Mostly fenced.

Of Note: This is not nearly as nice a park as nearby Serra or De Anza, but is a lot less used, so if solitude is what you're after, come here.

Walk 6: De Anza Park

Location: Lime Drive and Rockefeller Drive—easy to find. See Map 19.

Size: 10.5 acres, about three-quarters open grass

Parking: Lot off Rockefeller

For Comfort: Restrooms with wheelchair access, clean; water fountains; pay phone

For Sports: Softball field with bleachers, horseshoe pits

For Dining: 2 group areas, seating 60 and 140

For Kids: Playground, including "castle" with battlements, amusement-park type of suspended swings, and sculptured "rocks" for skateboarding

Description: Flat with a couple of small hills. Lush grass. Good shade areas. Lighted, paved path down length. Playground well used, but the remainder of the park fairly empty.

Of Note: The playground is a treat for everyone.

Walk 7: Las Palmas Park

Location: Danforth Drive and Russet Drive—easy to find. See Map 19.

Size: 6.5 acres originally, plus 10.4-acre addition; about three-quarters open space

Parking: Lots off Russet and Hyde Park

For Comfort: Restrooms with wheelchair access, clean; water fountains

For Sports: Municipal tennis center with 12 lighted courts and one unlighted court with bleachers

For Dining: 2 group areas, seating 40 each

For Kids: 2 playgrounds, one with a high fort, both under large palms and surrounded by a lagoon (now empty) .

Description: Rolling ground and small hills. Lush grass. Lighted, paved path around most of the perimeter. Nice shade areas. Tennis center building and recreation building. Unfenced. Quiet. Well used.

Of Note: This is a *big* park, and a walk around the perimeter is quite a good ramble.

Walk 8: Braly Park

Location: Daffodil Way off Gail Avenue—hard to find. See Map 19.

Size: 6.5 acres, about three-quarters open

Parking: Lot off Daffodil

For Comfort: Restrooms with wheelchair access, clean; water fountain

For Sports: 2 lighted tennis courts, horseshoe pits, shuffleboard

For Dining: 2 group areas, for 70 and 110 people

For Kids: Playground

Description: Mostly flat with a few small hills. Limited shade. Lighted, paved path around perimeter. Fenced except

across the front. In wetter times, there's a lagoon
around the playground area. Community building.

Of Note: This is smaller than other nearby parks, and harder to
find, but well kept and well used. It was positively
swarming with kids on my visit.

Walk 9: Ponderosa Park

Location: Iris Avenue off Wolfe Road—easy to find. See Map
19.

Size: 10 acres, about two-thirds open grass

Parking: Lot off Iris

For Comfort: Restrooms with wheelchair access, clean; water fountain

For Sports: 2 tennis courts, basketball court, sand volleyball
court, horseshoe pits, softball field, soccer field

For Dining: 2 group areas seating 68 each

For Kids: Playground built like a fort, complete with cannon and
"covered wagon"; bike racks

Description: Flat on the playing fields, otherwise rolling. Good
grass. Lighted, paved path winding through from one
corner to the opposite one. Good areas of shade.
Unfenced. Community building. Heavily used.

Of Note: The playing fields seem to be the most deserted area of
the park, but don't offer much shade.

Walk 10: Washington Park

Location: Pastoria Avenue and West Washington Avenue—
easy to find. See Map 19.

Size: 12 acres, nearly all open grass

Parking: Lots along Pastoria and Washington

For Comfort: Restrooms with wheelchair access, clean; water fountain

For Sports: 2 lighted tennis courts, lighted basketball courts, lighted softball field with bleachers, horseshoe pits, swimming pool

For Dining: 3 group areas, seating 180, 140 and 60

For Kids: Playground

Description: Flat with lush grass and a beautiful row of redwoods, plus other attractive trees. Lots of shade. Paved, lighted path around park near perimeter, excluding softball field. Community building.

Of Note: This park is next to the Senior Center, which also has a large lawn area.

Walk 11: Murphy Historical Park

Location: North Sunnyvale Avenue and California Avenue— easy to find. See Map 19.

Size: 5 acres, about half open grass

Parking: Lot on California

For Comfort: Restrooms with wheelchair access, clean; water fountains, pay phones

For Sports: Lawn bowling, horseshoe pits, shuffleboard

For Dining: 12 picnic tables, 6 barbecues

Description: Flat with the usual lush lawn. Paved, lighted path circles the park. Nice areas of shade under large old eucalyptus, palm, oak and willow. Some areas planted in flowers. Quiet. Community building. Outdoor log amphitheater.

Of Note: The historical museum has a sign that says it is open Tuesday 12–3:30, Thursday 12–3:30 and Sunday 1– 4, but I was there on Sunday during those hours and the museum was locked.

Walk 12: Fair Oaks Park

Location:	At Fair Oaks Avenue and Wolfe Road—easy to find. See Map 19.
Size:	18 acres, nearly all softball field
Parking:	Lot off Fair Oaks
For Comfort:	Restrooms with wheelchair access, clean; water fountain
For Sports:	2 softball fields with bleachers (1 lighted), 3 lighted volleyball courts, horseshoe pits
For Dining:	2 group areas, seating 120 and 64
Description:	Flat area nearly all taken up by softball fields. Very limited shade around edges and small front section. Lighted path part way across front. Community building.
Of Note:	This is not a very attractive park, and it had some broken glass and garbage around the parking lot. People in an RV appeared to be living in the parking lot.

Walk 13: Orchard Gardens Park

Location:	Garner Drive off Borregas Avenue—hard to find. See Map 19.
Size:	2 acres originally, plus 1-acre addition on other side of the street; about two-thirds open grass
Parking:	Neighborhood street parking
For Comfort:	Restrooms, reasonably clean; water fountain
For Sports:	2 tennis courts, basketball courts
For Dining:	3 picnic tables, 3 barbecues
For Kids:	Playground
Description:	Flat with good grass. Shade only around the edges. Paved, lighted path down length of park. Community building. Quiet.

Of Note: This one is rather small and definitely hard to get to. If you don't live within walking distance, choose another park.

Walk 14: Lakewood Park

Location: Silverlake Drive off Lakehaven Drive—easy to find. See Map 19.

Size: 16 acres, mostly open space

Parking: Lot on Lakechime

For Comfort: Restrooms with wheelchair access, clean; water fountains; pay phone

For Sports: 2 lighted tennis courts, lighted basketball courts, lighted handball courts, swimming pool, horseshoe pits, shuffleboard, lighted softball field with bleachers, 12 games tables

For Dining: 3 group areas to seat 60, 75 and 175

For Kids: Playground

Description: Few small hills, otherwise flat. Very lush grass. Paved, lighted path loops around most of park. Small stone amphitheater. Community building. Unfenced. Quiet.

Of Note: The paved path leads through the park and behind adjacent school grounds to Meadowlake Drive, a nice leisurely walk.

Walk 15: Fairwood Park

Location: Sandia Avenue off Lawrence Expwy.—easy to find. See Map 19.

Size: 1.6 acres, almost all open grass

Parking: Neighborhood street parking

For Comfort: Water fountain

For Dining: 1 group area to seat 40, 3 individual picnic tables with 3 barbecues

For Kids: 2 playground areas

Description: Small hills with lush grass. Paved, lighted path in oval around park. Fenced except on street side. Small amphitheater with upright log sections for seats.

Of Note: A loose German shepherd from the neighborhood was running around during my visit, so be aware.

Walk 16: Sunnyvale Baylands Park

Location: Moffett Park Drive and Lawrence Expwy.—easy to find. See Map 19.

Size: 237 acres county land, 100 acres city land; nearly all open, except for softball complex

Parking: Dead end street on Moffett Park

Description: Natural area of open marshlands and grasslands. Levee system for Santa Clara Water District. No formal trails. Lots of egrets and other waterbirds. Almost totally undeveloped area.

Of Note: The levees provide a fine series of walkways if you don't care to bushwhack across the marshes. Dogs are to be on leash, but you will likely meet many that aren't.

Chapter 8
Los Altos/Los Altos Hills

    Los Altos is second only to Campbell as Santa Clara County's city most unfriendly to dogs. Although there is no city ordinance barring dogs from parks, nearly all parks are individually signed to prohibit them. Some of the signing can be confusing. For example, McKenzie Park, which is really two small parks connected by a short path, has a sign in one section but not in the other.

    The only really worthwhile Los Altos park in which dogs are permitted is Redwood Grove Nature Preserve. Your dog must be on leash and you must clean up after him.

    Los Altos Hills offers the grasslands of Byrne Preserve for a sunny walk. Foothill College also allows dogs on campus. Be sure to clean up behind you and keep your dog on leash.

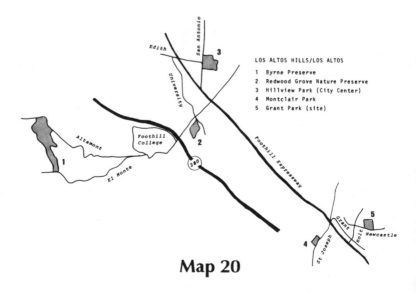

LOS ALTOS HILLS/LOS ALTOS

1 Byrne Preserve
2 Redwood Grove Nature Preserve
3 Hillview Park (City Center)
4 Montclair Park
5 Grant Park (site)

Map 20

Walk 1: Byrne Preserve (Los Altos Hills)

Location: Altamont Road—a little hard to find. See Map 20.

Size: Approximately 30 acres

Parking: At Westwind Farms barn opposite Black Mountain Road

For Comfort: Restrooms and water are in the barn

Description: Hilly natural grasslands with a few scattered trees for shade. Informal paths are mostly worn in by equestrians. You can walk, mostly in the sun, mostly up and down small hills, about one mile across to Moody Road.

Of Note: There are horses loose in the fields, as well as equestrians out for a ride, so be sure not to bother any of them. Foxtails and ticks can be large problems here. Horse trails also run along Black Mountain, Byrne Park, Taaffe and Altamont, and through Foothill College.

Walk 2: Redwood Grove Nature Preserve

Location: Off University Avenue between Sherman Street and Lincoln Avenue—watch for the sign. See Map 20.

Size: 5.5 acres, all open space

Parking: Neighborhood street parking

For Dining: 3 picnic tables

Description: A natural redwood grove and a seasonal stream. Boardwalks make a loop through and around the grove. Very shady and pleasant. Open meadow area around an old house. Sign warning visitors of poison oak.

Of Note: Definitely the best place in Los Altos you can go with a dog. A picnic table sitting by itself up some steps off the main path offers solitude and a good vantage point of the grove.

Walk 3: Hillview Park (City Center)

Location: San Antonio Road—easy to find. See Map 20.

Size: 6 acres, about two-thirds open space

Parking: 2 large lots off San Antonio

For Comfort: Restrooms and water fountains in various of the buildings

For Dining: 1 picnic table in the parking lot

For Kids: Playground

Description: City Center, with the city buildings, library and historical museum set amid an old orchard. Paved paths lead through the orchard to all the buildings. Not much shade.

Of Note: Since there are so few parks in Los Altos that allow dogs, you might want to bring yours here and be visible to the city fathers.

Walk 4: Montclair Park

Location: Stonehaven Drive off St. Joseph Avenue—easy to find. See Map 20.

Size: 1.1 acres, about one-quarter open space

Parking: Neighborhood street parking

For Comfort: Water fountain

For Sports: 2 tennis courts

For Dining: 4 picnic tables, 2 barbecues

For Kids: Small playground

Description: This is really a flat, nearly all paved area in front of a school yard, without much opportunity to walk anywhere but around in a circle. But if you want somewhere to have a picnic where you can take your dog in Los Altos, this is the place.

Of Note: With so few places to choose from in Los Altos, it may be this one or leave town.

Walk 5: Grant Park

Location: Holt Avenue off Grant Road—easy to find. See Map 20.

Size: 4.5 acres

Parking: Neighborhood street parking

Description: This is a recently closed school that will be converted to a park. Work on the grounds is scheduled for Spring 1990, renovation of the buildings for Winter 1991. Currently, it's mostly flat, with bare ground and weeds. NO DOGS ALLOWED signs posted at present.

Walk 6: A Miscellaneous Walk
Los Altos

Location: San Antonio Road. See Map 20.

Parking: Street parking, or the lot at the City Center, or various lots downtown

For Comfort: Restrooms and water fountains can be found in the buildings at City Center

For Dining: 1 picnic table in lot at City Center

Description: You can start with some window shopping downtown, or make yourself and your dog visible to the city government at City Center. Either way, you can walk along San Antonio toward Mountain View for about a mile. There are sidewalks on both sides of the street, mostly buffered from the road by a planting strip, and often shaded by large, attractive trees. There is almost always traffic along San Antonio, but you are not directly alongside it, and the noise is not too horrendous. The homes are attractive, and the path mostly shady.

Walk 7: Foothill College

Location: El Monte Road—easy to find. See Map 20.

Size: None given by college—large

Parking: Lot for public and students at the bottom of the hill; be sure to get a permit from one of the red dispensers for 50¢ if it's a weekday

For Comfort: Restrooms in various buildings; water fountains

For Sports: Parcourse

Description: The campus sits on a hill, so most paths are up and down, but at least part of the dirt parcourse track is fairly level. Lots of trees, so plenty of shade. Fairly quiet, but watch for traffic when you're near any of the parking lots.

Of Note: The campus can offer quite a ramble, and is good for a day when it's too hot to tackle the sunny expanse of Byrne Preserve.

Chapter 9
Mountain View

Like most cities in Santa Clara County, Mountain View has leash and clean-up laws. However, it also has two rather unusual developments. One is a "school park." There are actually two kinds: the first is a school yard that is opened for public use whenever school is not in session; the second has a park area separate from the school yard that can be used on all days but is larger on nonschool days because you can use the school yard. Those composed entirely of school yards mostly lack trees and any sort of landscaping. But if you just want a place for some exercise, they're fine.

The second arrangement is a very welcome one. For dog owners engaged in obedience training, Mountain View issues permits allowing them to practice off-leash work in public parks. Of course, dogs must be under control. Congratulations to Mountain View on such an enlightened policy. Here's hoping other cities follow suit.

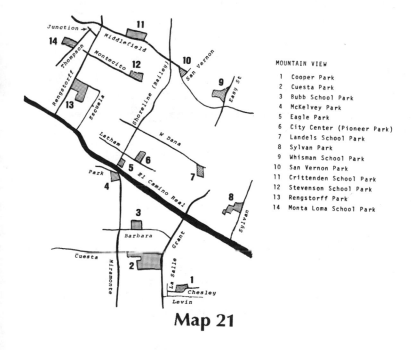

MOUNTAIN VIEW

1   Cooper Park
2   Cuesta Park
3   Bubb School Park
4   McKelvey Park
5   Eagle Park
6   City Center (Pioneer Park)
7   Landels School Park
8   Sylvan Park
9   Whisman School Park
10 San Vernon Park
11 Crittenden School Park
12 Stevenson School Park
13 Rengstorff Park
14 Monta Loma School Park

Map 21

Walk 1: Cooper Park

Location:	Chesley Avenue off Levin Avenue—a little hard to find. See Map 21.
Size:	11 acres, nearly all open grass
Parking:	Neighborhood street parking
For Comfort:	Restrooms with wheelchair access, clean; water fountains
For Sports:	4 tennis courts, 2 softball fields
For Dining:	3 small tables
For Kids:	Playgrounds, bike racks
Description:	Slightly rolling, with good grass. Nice shade areas. Paved, lighted path across width. Quiet. Unfenced.
Of Note:	This is quite an appealing park, and doesn't seem to be much used.

Walk 2: Cuesta Park

Location:	Cuesta Drive and Grant Road—easy to find. See Map 21.
Size:	32 acres, nearly all open grass
Parking:	Several large lots off Cuesta
For Comfort:	Restrooms with wheelchair access, clean; water fountains
For Sports:	Tennis center with 12 lighted courts with bleachers, 2 lighted handball courts, horseshoe pits, volleyball court
For Dining:	4 group areas with large barbecues; 7 individual picnic tables, 7 barbecues
For Kids:	2 playground areas
Description:	Some flat land, some rolling hills. Very lush grass. Good areas of shade and sun with a fine variety of trees. Plenty of sunny lawns. Lighted, paved path winding around and through the park.

Of Note: A big park that's just about perfect for almost everyone. Lots of people know about it, and there are kids
and dogs, roller skaters, skateboarders, bicyclists, and
just about anyone else you can think of, making their
way through the park or relaxing in the sun.

Walk 3: Bubb School Park

Location: Barbara Avenue off Grant Road—easy to find. See
Map 21.

Size: 9 acres, nearly all open grass

Parking: Lot on weekends only, otherwise neighborhood street
parking

For Comfort: Water fountain

For Sports: Softball field with bleachers

For Dining: 4 small tables

For Kids: Playground

Description: Flat area with limited shade in front of the school.
Farther down is an area that is not part of the school
yard and is available as a park during the week. This
area has some nice shade trees.

Of Note: Although the full 9 acres is available only when school
is not in session, the "park" area is quite pleasant.

Walk 4: McKelvey Ball Park

Location: Park Drive off Miramonte Avenue—easy to find. See Map 21.

Size: 5 acres, all open grass

Parking: Lot off Park

For Comfort: Water fountain

For Sports: Lighted softball field with bleachers

Description: Large, flat, open field. Fenced. No shade to speak of. Paved path leads from parking lot to field only.

Of Note: This is really just a softball field and nothing more.

Walk 5: Eagle Park

Location: High School Way and Franklin Street—easy to find. See Map 21.

Size: 6 acres, about three-quarters open grass

Parking: Small, crowded lot on Franklin, less used lot on Church Street

For Comfort: Restrooms with wheelchair access, sparkling clean; water fountains

For Sports: Lighted swimming pool

For Dining: 7 picnic tables

For Kids: Playground

Description: Fairly flat. Grass in the large open area is a bit weedy. No shade to speak of. Dirt path around swim center/playground area. Quiet. Unfenced.

Of Note: This is a fairly new park, dedicated November 11, 1989. There are attractive portals and a small plaza with flowers and a dedication plaque. Seems to be favored by city workers at lunchtime.

Walk 6: Pioneer Memorial Park

Location: Franklin and Church streets—easy to find. See Map 21.

Size: 5 acres, about two-thirds open grass

Parking: Neighborhood street parking

For Comfort: Restrooms and water fountains in various buildings

Description: Slightly hilly with lush grass. City offices and library are mostly at back of area. Front is large lawn with mature trees and attractive planted area. Paved path winds across.

Of Note: A massive construction project in the area currently has traffic in an uproar and makes the entire block rather unpleasant. But once the building is finished, this will return to being an appealing, shady park with limited parking.

Walk 7: Landels School Park

Location: West Dana Street near Highway 85—easy to find. See Map 21.

Size: 10 acres, nearly all open grass

Parking: Weekend-only lot on West Dana, otherwise limited street parking

For Sports: Basketball courts, softball field

Description: Flat area with good grass. Some shade, mostly around the edges. Paved path through school buildings only.

Of Note: The fields are behind the school buildings, and the lot is full and off-limits on school days, so this really is a park only on the weekends.

Walk 8: Sylvan Park

Location: Sylvan Avenue off El Camino Real—easy to find. See Map 21.

Size: 9 acres, about three-quarters open grass

Parking: Small lot off Sylvan

For Comfort: Restrooms with wheelchair access, clean; water fountains

For Sports: 8 game tables, horseshoe pits, fitness center, 4 tennis courts

For Dining: 6 picnic tables, 4 barbecues

For Kids: Playground

Description: Mostly flat with a few small hills. Good grass, and nice landscaping. Paved path meandering around. No appreciable shade. Quiet. Unfenced.

Of Note: There are odd little corners of park sticking out to meet various streets, making for small pockets of more private grass.

Walk 9: Whisman School Park

Location: Easy Street off Middlefield Road—easy to find. See Map 21.

Size: 12 acres, nearly all open grass

Parking: Lot off Easy

For Comfort: Restrooms with wheelchair access, clean; water fountain

For Sports: 4 tennis courts, softball field with bleachers, fitness apparatus

For Dining: 14 picnic tables, 7 barbecues

For Kids: Playground

Description: Mostly rolling, with nice grass. Lots of small areas of shade. Fenced except for street side. Paved path loops through length of park. More-natural dirt area at back, with inaccessible concrete-lined stream running behind.

Of Note: This is the nicest of the school parks, and open for use not just on weekends, as some of them are.

Walk 10: San Vernon Park

Location:	San Vernon Avenue and Middlefield Road—easy to find. See Map 21.
Size:	2 acres, nearly all open grass
Parking:	Neighborhood street parking
For Comfort:	Water fountain
For Sports:	Basketball court
For Kids:	Playground
Description:	One medium hill with some flatter ground around it. Nice grass. Paved path circling around and through the park. Some traffic noise from Middlefield. Low fence along most of Middlefield side.
Of Note:	This is a small but attractive park, probably best suited for those who live nearby.

Walk 11: Crittenden School Park

Location:	Middlefield Road between Terra Bella Avenue and Rengstorff Avenue—easy to find. See Map 21.
Size:	15 acres, nearly all open grass
Parking:	Large lot off Middlefield, only open on weekends
For Comfort:	Restrooms, reasonably clean; water fountain
For Sports:	2 lighted softball fields, basketball courts, parcourse
For Kids:	Playground
Description:	Flat, with entire park fenced, and one softball field separately fenced. Not much shade. Paved path along parking lot and half of one side of softball field only. Some traffic noise.
Of Note:	This park reflects Mountain View's philosophy that during the week it's to be used by the school and on the weekends by the public. If the parking lot isn't open, the nearest parking is about a block away amid businesses on a side street.

Walk 12: Stevenson School Park

Location: Montecito Avenue off Shoreline Blvd.—easy to find. See Map 21.

Size: 12 acres, all open

Parking: Neighborhood street parking

For Sports: Softball field

Description: Flat, open field with good grass. Some limited shade along one side. Fenced. No path. Not all that attractive.

Of Note: This is another of Mountain View's school parks, but without much to recommend it. Others are more attractive and offer more variety.

Walk 13: Rengstorff Park

Location: Leland Avenue and Rengstorff Avenue—easy to find. See Map 21.

Size: 27 acres, about three-quarters open grass

Parking: Lot off Leland, lot off Rengstorff

For Comfort: Restrooms with wheelchair access, clean; water fountains

For Sports: Parcourse, swimming pool, handball courts, volleyball court, soccer field, fitness cluster, 8 lighted tennis courts with judges' chairs and bleachers

For Dining: Large group area, can be reserved daily from May through September, with Mountain View businesses and residents given preference

For Kids: 3 playgrounds—1 small, 1 open to the public on weekends only, 1 large with no dogs allowed

Description: Mostly flat, with some small hills. Nice grass and beautiful large trees. Nice areas of sun and shade. Lighted, paved paths running all through park. Fairly quiet. Mostly fenced. Beautifully clean.

Of Note: A large park where you can have quite a nice walk. Can be crowded on weekends.

Walk 14: Monta Loma School Park

Location: Thompson Avenue between Central Expwy. and Middlefield Road—easy to find. See Map 21.

Size: 7 acres, nearly all open grass

Parking: Neighborhood street parking

For Comfort: Restrooms open for scheduled activities only; water fountain

For Sports: Softball field with bleachers, 3 game tables

For Dining: 2 picnic tables

For Kids: 2 playgrounds

Description: Flat, including large area with very nice grass. Lighted, paved path along avenue of trees runs through length of park and across width to school. Not much shade. Unfenced. Quiet.

Of Note: The lush green area with the row of trees marching away down its length is visually appealing. The park was one of the few I've found empty.

Chapter 10
Palo Alto

Palo Alto is a fine place to walk with a dog. Not only are you both allowed in all parks, but three parks include fenced exercise areas, where your dog can run off leash. The largest of these is in Mitchell Park, and comes complete with tennis balls left by regular visitors. For those who live or work in Palo Alto (or can arrange to be accompanied by someone who does), Foothills Park offers a vast natural area for hiking, boating, or just relaxing in the foothills. A smaller park in the same area, Foothills Open Space Preserve, is open to all, and allows leashed dogs on the trail.

There is a relaxing air about Palo Alto. Just driving through the neighborhoods admiring the houses is enjoyable. Be sure to obey the speed limits, as the Palo Alto police take them very seriously. Also keep an eye out for the black squirrels of Palo Alto. They're a local color variation, and some do indeed appear to be jet black.

Outside the special exercise areas, the usual leash and clean-up laws apply.

Walk 1: Esther Clark Park

Location:	Old Adobe Road in foothills—a little hard to find. See Map 22.
Size:	21.72 acres, all open natural meadow
Parking:	Along curb at dead end
Description:	This is an undeveloped park. Open sloping meadow with dirt tracks across. Small stream accessible at bottom. Few trees for shade in the front corner. Used by equestrians. Quiet. Sits amid some fine homes.
Of Note:	If you want to be in a fairly natural area but you don't like woods and closed-in trails, this could be the place for you. Also, if you like to look at expensive houses, they're all around the meadow.

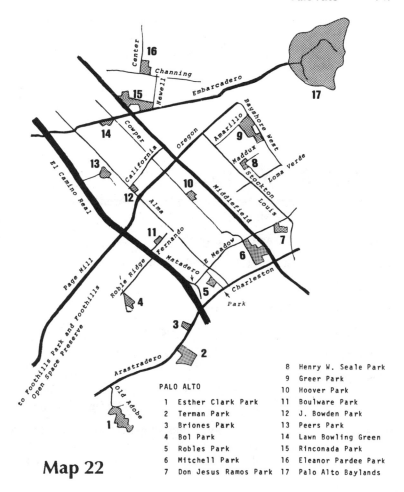

Map 22

PALO ALTO

1   Esther Clark Park
2   Terman Park
3   Briones Park
4   Bol Park
5   Robles Park
6   Mitchell Park
7   Don Jesus Ramos Park
8   Henry W. Seale Park
9   Greer Park
10 Hoover Park
11 Boulware Park
12 J. Bowden Park
13 Peers Park
14 Lawn Bowling Green
15 Rinconada Park
16 Eleanor Pardee Park
17 Palo Alto Baylands

Walk 2: Terman Park

Location: Access road off Arastradero Road—a little hard to spot. See Map 22.

Size: About 4.7 acres are in open grass

Parking: Lot off Arastradero

For Comfort: Water fountain

For Sports: 8 tennis courts, swimming pool, 2 soccer fields, softball field, basketball court

Description: Flat, mostly open playing fields. Nice grass. Limited shade around edges. Path only around library and other buildings. Sits behind whole complex of library, Jewish Community Center, swimming center.

Of Note: Unless you know this one, the entrance is rather hard to see as you're driving by, and it's really just an open field.

Walk 3: Briones Park

Location: Arastradero Road and Clemo Avenue—easy to find. See Map 22.

Size: 4.1 acres, nearly all open space

Parking: Street parking on dead end

For Comfort: Water fountain

For Sports: Basketball court

For Dining: 8 picnic tables, 4 barbecues

For Kids: 2 large playgrounds (no dogs in one)

Description: Fairly flat, with grass burned only in the sunniest places. Good areas of shade. Dirt path around the park (muddy in wet weather). Unfenced. Quiet.

Of Note: The lights, playground equipment, and a bridge are all constructed of logs and make for a lot of visual interest in this park. However, it's rather sloppy walking, even on the path, after a rain.

Walk 4: Bol Park

Location: Laguna Avenue off Los Robles Avenue—a little hard to find. See Map 22.

Size: About 5 acres, all open

Parking: Lot along Laguna

For Comfort: Water fountain

For Sports: Horseshoe pits

For Kids: Small playground

Description: Slightly rolling open meadow along stream. Dirt path down one side, with semihidden steps down to the stream at one point. Lighted concrete pathway with dirt shoulders runs along opposite side of park, and continues in both directions, much favored by joggers and walkers.

Of Note: You can really choose your walk here—a long ramble on the paved jogging path, a shorter walk along the dirt path. Or you can sit on the benches conveniently placed on the bridge over the water and watch the stream go by and the burro play in the adjacent field. Or you can go down to the stream itself and sit in the shade while your dog plays in the water.

Walk 5: Robles Park

Location: Park Blvd.—easy to find. See Map 22.

Size: 4.65 acres, nearly all open

Parking: Neighborhood street parking

For Comfort: Water fountain

For Sports: Basketball court, softball field

For Dining: 3 picnic tables, 2 barbecues

For Kids: Playground

Description: Relatively flat, with grass mostly burned out. Dirt path around about half the park. Good shade trees.

Probably normally quiet, but construction at house on one side was making it unpleasantly noisy during my visit.

Of Note: Somehow not as attractive as most of Palo Alto's parks, perhaps because of the brown grass.

Walk 6: Mitchell Park

Location: East Meadow Drive—easy to find. See Map 22.

Size: 20 acres, nearly all open

Parking: Lot off East Meadow

For Comfort: Restrooms, clean; water fountains

For Sports: 2 giant people-size chess boards, 7 game tables, 7 lighted tennis courts, 2 clay tennis courts, 4 handball courts, horseshoe pits, shuffleboard, 2 soccer fields, softball field, measured ½-mile run on dirt around park

For Dining: 30 picnic tables, 27 barbecues

For Kids: Wading pool (closed on my visit), playground with bear sculptures for kids to climb on (no dogs)

Description: Flat with some small hills. Lots of shade. Dirt and paved paths, one measured for ½-mile run. Lots of benches and tables. Plaque and small redwood where landmark redwood El Palo Alto for which town is named once stood. Quiet. Even the city sculpture is interesting.

Of Note: This park has the largest of the dog-run areas, more than twice as big as the other two. There are tennis balls left in the area to play with, and there's quite a social gathering weekday mornings. To reach the dog run, drive to the back of the parking lot and walk toward the softball field—it will be on your left.

Walk 7: Don Jesus Ramos Park

Location: East Meadow Drive—easy to find. See Map 22.

Size: 3.56 acres, nearly all open space

Parking: Neighborhood street parking

For Comfort: Water fountain

For Sports: Basketball court

For Dining: 8 picnic tables, 4 barbecues

For Kids: Playground

Description: Flat with good grass. Benches and picnic tables in shade under trees. Paved path loops in oval around inside of park. Fenced except on street side. Quiet. Some nice landscaping.

Of Note: This park—like most of Palo Alto's parks—has the type of fountain without a catch basin, so that even short dogs can have a drink.

Walk 8: Henry W. Seale Park

Location: Stockton Place and Maddux Drive—a little hard to find. See Map 22.

Size: 3.24 acres, nearly all open

Parking: Neighborhood street parking

For Comfort: Water fountain

For Sports: Basketball court

For Dining: 6 picnic tables, 3 barbecues

For Kids: Playground

Description: Flat except for one tiny hill. Okay grass, burning slightly in some areas. Decent amount of shade. Dirt path across width. Open field area hidden around corner behind playground. Quiet. Unobtrusive landscaping.

Of Note: This is one of the few parks that I found totally deserted.

Walk 9: Greer Park

Location: Amarillo Avenue at West Bayshore Road—easy to find. See Map 22.

Size: 4.98 acres is what is given by the city, but this park is bigger than that, and nearly all open

Parking: Lot off Bayshore

For Comfort: Restrooms, clean; water fountains

For Sports: Basketball court, 3 softball fields, soccer field

For Dining: 6 picnic tables, 3 barbecues

For Kids: 2 playground areas (dogs not allowed in one)

Description: Flat except for one small hill, with grass that's just hanging in there during the drought. Lighted, paved path makes small loop around playgrounds and restrooms only. Several shade areas. Quiet.

Of Note: This is one of Palo Alto's three dog-run parks. The run here is grass, fenced off from the rest of the park, where dogs can be let off leash. Front gate is generally locked, but back is unlocked. About a quarter acre area in the run.

Walk 10: Hoover Park

Location: Cowper Street between Colorado Avenue and Loma Verde Avenue—easy to find. See Map 22.

Size: 4.19 acres, about three-quarters open

Parking: Neighborhood street parking

For Comfort: Water fountain

For Sports: 2 tennis courts, handball courts, softball field, basketball court

For Dining: 6 picnic tables, 2 barbecues

For Kids: Playground

Description: In wetter times a little stream runs down one side. Some areas are flat, some rolling. The grass is burning in the drought. Paved path down length. Most attractive in the stream area, with portals with lights arching above the path, and the rock course of the stream.

Of Note: This is another dog-run park. This run is just dirt and trees, with a couple of benches for owners. There is also an interesting drawing of a man and a dog on the side of the handball courts.

Walk 11: Boulware Park

Location: Ash Street and Fernando Avenue—easy if you come in from. El Camino, but don't try from another direction. See Map 22.

Size: 1.48 acres, nearly all open

Parking: Neighborhood street parking

For Comfort: Water fountain

For Sports: Basketball court

For Dining: 4 picnic tables, 2 barbecues

For Kids: 2 playgrounds

Description: Flat, with okay grass. A good amount of shade. Paved path around. Quiet.

Of Note: This park is small and can be nearly impossible to find if you approach from the wrong direction. Best to go somewhere else.

Walk 12: Bowden Park

Location: California Avenue and Alma Street—easy to find. See Map 22.

Size: 2 acres, about three-quarters open

Parking: Lot on High St.

For Dining: 6 small tables, with 4 under a shade gazebo

For Kids: Playground

Description: Small hills with lots of trees and shade. Plenty of benches. Partly paved path runs down length. Lots of traffic noise.

Of Note: This is a small but attractive park. You can reach it on foot from the other side of Alma via a pedestrian undercrossing.

Walk 13: Peers Park

Location: Park Blvd.—a little hard to find. See Map 22.

Size: 4.70 acres, nearly all open

Parking: Neighborhood street parking

For Comfort: Restrooms, clean; water fountain

For Sports: 2 tennis courts, basketball court

For Dining: 5 picnic tables

For Kids: Playground (no dogs allowed)

Description: Flat, with badly burned grass. Several large trees for shade. Paved path across front and through width. Some traffic noise.

Of Note: Park Blvd. is a tricky road, which does not go through as maps show. Approach the park from the Page Mill side, as closely as possible.

Walk 14: Lawn Bowling Green

Location: Cowper Street and Churchill Avenue—easy to find. See Map 22.

Size: 1.87 acres, about one-third open grass

Parking: Lot on Churchill

For Comfort: Water fountain

For Sports: Lawn bowling

Description: Flat, with the grass outside the lawn bowling area mostly burned. Nice shade with some benches.

Traffic noise from nearby Embarcadero. Next to Elizabeth Gamble Garden Center.

Of Note: This park is really mostly taken up by the lawn-bowling area, but if you like to watch, it's a pleasant enough place.

Walk 15: Rinconada Park

Location: Embarcadero Road and Newell Road—easy to find. See Map 22.

Size: 19 acres, about three-quarters open grass

Parking: Lot on Hopkins Avenue

For Comfort: Restrooms, clean; water fountains

For Sports: 6 lighted tennis courts, lighted swimming pool, shuffleboard

For Dining: 12 picnic tables, 9 barbecues

For Kids: Playground, bike racks

Description: Mostly flat, with nice lawn. Lots of shade, including shade gazebo with benches. Paved pavilion area. Paved, lighted path loops around and through park. Small commemorative redwood grove on Hopkins side. Quiet. Unfenced. Cultural Center, with more lawn, on one side, school on the other.

Of Note: The redwood grove is very pleasant, especially on a hot day. The trees' shade is refreshing and they smell wonderful.

Walk 16: Eleanor Pardee Park

Location: Center Drive at Channing Avenue—easy to find. See Map 22.

Size: 10 acres, nearly all open, some natural

Parking: Neighborhood street parking

For Comfort: Water fountain

For Dining: 6 picnic tables, 3 barbecues

For Kids: Playground (no dogs allowed)

Description: Slightly rolling with nice grass in most of park, seminatural area at end past picnic tables. Paved path loops around. Beautiful huge eucalyptus trees provide shade. Several other trees have grown with their trunks nearly parallel to the ground. Circular paved pavilion. Quiet.

Of Note: There are two or three trees here that can actually be walked up, their trunks are so slanting.

Walk 17: Palo Alto Baylands
(Yacht Harbor)

Location: End of Embarcadero Road—easy to find. See Map 22.

Size: 121 acres, nearly all open

Parking: Various lots

For Comfort: Portable toilets at duck pond; restrooms and water fountain in Interpretive Center

For Sports: Fishing

Description: Mostly natural baylands area includes boat launch, duck pond, and Interpretive Center. Boardwalk leads out across marsh (a tape recording is available for the blind when the Interpretive Center is open). Levees lead around various parts of the marsh. One levee leads almost to the runway of Palo Alto's municipal airport, and there's always plenty of activity for plane buffs. What was once the yacht harbor is now an area of mud with a few small boats left stuck in it.

Of Note: Dogs seem to prefer walking on the levees to the boardwalk. The smells are probably better, and there are ground squirrels everywhere. The Interpretive Center is open Sat. and Sun. 1 to 5, and Wed. through Fri. 2 to 5.

Walk 18: Foothills Park

Location: Page Mill Road about 2½ miles south of 280—easy to find, but the road is winding, so use caution. See Map 22.

Size: 1400 acres, nearly all either open meadow or natural woodland

Parking: Various lots within the park

For Comfort: Restrooms, clean; water fountains

For Sports: Fishing, boating (non-motorized, hand-launched only)

For Dining: 7 picnic areas (1 can be reserved)

Description: Sometimes gentle, sometimes steep foothills, with large lake in meadow surrounded by natural terrain. There are streams, rugged brush country, oak forest and grasslands. Hiking trails cover 15 miles, and range from a gentle self-guided nature trail to a 7½-mile outing.

Of Note: Only Palo Alto residents and their guests are permitted in this park. If you are not a resident or accompanied by one, you will be turned away. Dogs are permitted only on weekdays and must be kept on leash.

Walk 19: Foothills Open-Space Preserve

Location: Page Mill Road, about 3½ miles south of 280—somewhat hard to find. See Map 22.

Size: 181 acres, all open and natural

Parking: Room for 2 cars at pullout along wood rail fence with brown pipe gate and sign FIRE LANE. On opposite side of road from Palo Alto Foothills Park entrance and about 1 mile farther on.

Description: Grassy ridgetop surrounded by steep slopes covered in chaparral. Oak and madrone woodland in the valleys. Trail leads up approximately ½ mile to knoll with fine view of the area. Trail then becomes narrow and drops steeply down to Hidden Villa Ranch. Trail is partly in sun, partly in shade. Becomes muddy fairly quickly in rain.

Of Note: You can have a good workout here with your dog, especially if you continue past the knoll. Unfortunately, there are broken glass and litter on the trail, mostly in the vicinity of the knoll. Also take precautions against ticks. If you come in the rain, as I did, you're more likely to find a parking space, but be careful because the trail is slippery. The clouds hanging in the hills are beautiful then, though.

Walk 20: Miscellaneous Walk #1 Palo Alto

Location: Arastradero Road between Alpine Road and Page Mill Expwy.

Parking: Small lot at each end

Description: Start from the west about ½ mile from Alpine, or from the east about ½ mile from Page Mill. The sign for the trail is tucked along the roadside. Keep a careful watch.

From the west, you walk beside a lively little stream, with a bit of an uphill climb. You are restricted to the trail right-of-way, but there is open land all around, for a nice spacious feel. Other than a short stretch under old eucalyptuses, the trail is mostly in the sun, so in summer a morning or evening stroll is probably best. At the end, the trail returns to the stream and a small meadow, where you may see quail scurrying about their business.

The trail is one mile one way.

Walk 21: Miscellaneous Walk #2
Palo Alto

Location: Gunn High School at Foothill Expwy. and Arastradero Road or Bol Park (see p. 149).

Parking: Lot at Gunn High School (difficult on school days), lot at Bol Park

Description: From the high school, take the path with the tennis courts on your right. An old railway right-of-way will lead you to Matadero Creek and into Bol Park. There are benches here where you can sit and contemplate the creek. The path continues out the other side of the park as a narrower trail through some trees. It ends at Hanover Road, nearly 1½ miles one way.

On the return trip, you can follow the dirt trail on the creek side of Bol Park, recross the bridge over Matadero Creek, and take a left onto a second path, which will return you to Gunn High School by a slightly different route. A 3-mile walk without retracing your steps for more than maybe ¼ mile is certainly a rarity within a city, and the route is well used by joggers, bicyclists and people just getting from one place to another.

Walk 22: Miscellaneous Walk #3
Palo Alto

Location: Arastradero Road opposite Gunn High School (near Foothill) at one end, Mercedes Avenue in Los Altos at the other.

Description: A sign BIKE PATH TO LOS ALTOS marks the start of the path across the street from Gunn High School. It runs along Alta Mesa Cemetery at first, following the right-of-way for the Hetch Hetchy aqueduct. The bridge over Adobe Creek marks the boundary between Palo Alto and Los Altos.

The pavement ends before you reach Mercedes, but a narrower, unpaved path continues along the aqueduct. The entire trail is fairly level and mostly in sun, and is almost exactly one mile one way.

Walk 23: Miscellaneous Walk #4
Palo Alto

Location: Arastradero Road west of Foothill at one end, Purissima Road at Highway 280 in Los Altos Hills at the other.

Description: At the BIKE PATH sign, a paved path begins. It makes a gradual rise as it passes several industrial parks, then dips down to run beside Deer Creek. Here you are generally walking past the horses that graze these meadows, mostly in the sun.

Since this path is meant primarily for bicyclists, be sure to see that you and your dog do not block the path. Keep to one side and be alert for those approaching you from behind.

Walk 24: A Miscellaneous Walk
Stanford University

Location: El Camino Real or Junipero Serra Blvd.—easy to find.

Size: Hundreds of acres, some the official campus and some "Stanford lands," grasslands

Parking: Various lots throughout the campus

For Comfort: Water fountains and restrooms in some buildings

Description: The campus includes the main approach through rows of palm trees, open fields, and shady wooded areas. Paths seem to run everywhere. The Stanford lands are many, many acres of hills fronting Highway 280, some with cattle grazing on them. There are public access points along Junipero Serra, and you can walk your dog here.

Of Note: On the campus, you stand about equal chances of being run down by bicycles or mobbed by students who miss their own dogs. On the open hills, beware of ticks and keep your dog on leash. Formerly, this regulation was left unenforced, but people have recently been stopped and fined.

Chapter 11
County and Open-Space Areas

Regulations here can be confusing. Dogs are permitted or not on an area-by-area basis. County parks officials informed me that dogs were allowed in all areas of Uvas Canyon County Park, but on my arrival I was greeted with NO DOGS ALLOWED ON TRAIL signs everywhere. Conversation with a ranger confirmed that the signs were correct and the county officials weren't. All information in this section is based on what was found at the site itself, even if that contradicts what was printed elsewhere.

Many of the county parks are based around reservoirs. The drought has had a major effect on these areas. One was temporarily closed, others have specific areas closed. Caution should be used when approaching the water's edge, as receding waters can leave behind ground which appears to be solid but is actually a quagmire with a thin covering of dried mud.

The Midpeninsula Open Space District has many fine areas, but only a couple are open to dogs, and these only recently. If we behave in particularly exemplary fashion, perhaps more of these delightful spaces will become available to dogs and their owners.

Visits to many of these parks involve long, often winding drives, so plan to spend some time at the park to make it worthwhile. Pack a picnic, carry water, and relax and enjoy the countryside.

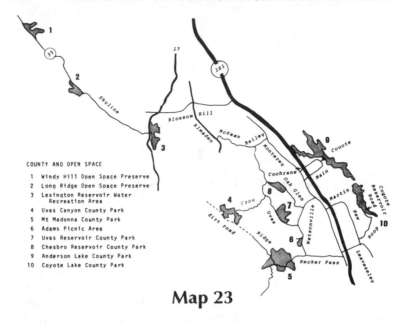

COUNTY AND OPEN SPACE

1 Windy Hill Open Space Preserve
2 Long Ridge Open Space Preserve
3 Lexington Reservoir Water
   Recreation Area
4 Uvas Canyon County Park
5 Mt Madonna County Park
6 Adams Picnic Area
7 Uvas Reservoir County Park
8 Chesbro Reservoir County Park
9 Anderson Lake County Park
10 Coyote Lake County Park

Map 23

Walk 1: Windy Hill Open Space Preserve

Location: Skyline Blvd. south of old La Honda Road—the picnic area is the easiest to find. See Map 23.

Size: 1,130 acres, all natural open space

Parking: Small pullout on the left as you come from 84 at a wood rail fence and brown pipe gate with FIRE LANE and small preserve sign; larger, more formal lot about ¼ mile up the road, with trail sign and picnic tables.

Description: From the first pulloff, the Spring Ridge Trail goes straight ahead, fairly flat at first, then winding down the hillsides. It has several options farther along, including one that leads past Sausal Pond, about 2½ miles in. The Anniversary Trail goes uphill to the right. It climbs for the first ¼ mile or so, then mostly levels off, with side trails leading to the tops of hills. It leads about ¾ mile to the picnic area. You can return to the start along the road if you want a different walk. The Anniversary Trail is not for those afraid of open spaces, as it is carved into the flank of the hill. To walk from the picnic area, consult the trail map there. The

Anniversary Trail will set out to your left, and connect with the Spring Ridge Trail.

Of Note: This is not called Windy Hill without reason. It's 1900 feet in elevation, and the wind almost always blows. Bring a jacket. Keep to these two trails, as that's where dogs are permitted.

Walk 2: Long Ridge Open Space Preserve

Location: Skyline Blvd. about 3 miles north of Saratoga Gap—a little hard to locate the exact spot. See Map 23.

Size: 980 acres, all natural open space

Parking: Large pullout at Grizzly Flat, across Skyline from a pullout with a sign for Upper Stevens Creek County Park

Description: A series of grassy ridges. Trail leads down around one ridge and into woodland in a ravine. Dogs are allowed only in the designated "Grizzly Flat" area, but there is no formal marking about where to stop. The map from Midpeninsula District shows as legal a long, narrow area across the front of the preserve. It's probably best to keep to the grassy hills and stay out of the woods, as they are probably out of bounds. During our midday visit, we saw two pairs of deer, who bounded off a little way and stopped to watch us.

Of Note: Midpeninsula District recommends calling them before visiting this preserve, as access conditions may change. The number is 415/949-5500.

Walk 3: Lexington Reservoir Water Recreation Area

Location: Alma Bridge Road off Highway 17—easy to find. See Map 23.

Size: The county is not forthcoming with the acreage of its parks, but all in this section are of quite substantial size

Parking:	Lot above dam
For Sports:	When there is water in the reservoir, there are fishing and boating, and workouts of the Santa Clara University crew teams, but that condition hasn't existed for several years
Description:	A reservoir surrounded by grassy hillsides. For now, the area around the reservoir is closed to the public while Santa Clara County and the Santa Clara Water District try to decide on the future of this space. You can still park in the lot and hike away from the reservoir on either the Los Gatos Creek Trail, which ends at the dam, or the St. Josephs Hill Trail, which has a trailhead just a short way up the road from the dam.
Of Note:	Keep an eye on the local papers for information on when events start occurring here. There was talk at one time about a fancy restaurant and all sorts of water sports, but that idea went away with the water.

Walk 4: Uvas Canyon County Park

Location:	Croy Road off Uvas Road—easy to find if you consult a map. See Map 23.
Parking:	Lots at picnic grounds
For Comfort:	Restrooms, clean; water fountains
For Dining:	Several picnic areas
Description:	Wooded hillside and a canyon with a lively stream. The picnic areas are fairly large, and the campground also. Camping is $8 per night plus $1 per dog, with a maximum of 2 dogs per site. Dogs must be inside the tent or car during the night.
Of Note:	Although the county told me that dogs were allowed in all areas of this park, it is heavily signed against dogs. They are permitted only in campgrounds and picnic areas and along the road. I asked one ranger if, where the stream crosses the road, you could step off the road a foot or two and allow your dog to get his feet wet. The answer was no.

The road in is fairly winding, and goes through the Sveadal Improvement Center just before reaching the park.

Walk 5: Mt. Madonna County Park

Location: Off Hecker Pass Road—easy to find. See Map 23.

Parking: At picnic areas and campsites

For Comfort: Restrooms, clean; water fountains

For Dining: Picnic tables, barbecues, firewood for sale

Description: Heavily wooded hill, with open meadows near the top. A large deer pen with quite a nice little herd sits next to one picnic area. Valley View Road leads to a pond and a campground, but is closed in winter. The main campground remains open. Camping is $8 per night plus $1 per dog, with a maximum of 2 dogs per site. Dogs must be kept in the tent or the car at night. There is a second access to the bottom of the hill on the Morgan Hill side, with a seasonal stream.

Of Note: Dogs are allowed only in the campgrounds and day-use areas and along the roads, but this encompasses a huge area. The campgrounds are quite large, so are the picnic areas, and there are miles of roads. You can have quite a good time here.

Walk 6: Adams Picnic Area

Location: Watsonville Road between Uvas Reservoir and Hecker Pass Road—easy to find. See Map 23.

Size: Approximately 4 acres

Parking: Large turnout

For Comfort: Portable toilets, water fountain

For Dining: Picnic tables, barbecues

Description: From the road, you see picnic tables set in a meadow with trees behind them. If you walk away from the road, you find an embankment leading down to a very

	pleasant stream, more picnic tables, and some truly massive rock outcroppings you can climb on.
Of Note:	The lower area along the stream would make a fine spot for a summer picnic, cool and shady.

Walk 7: Uvas Reservoir

Location:	Uvas Road—easy to find. See Map 23.
Parking:	Lot at boat launch area
For Sports:	Usually boating and fishing, but boating has been suspended during the drought
Description:	A reservoir with grassy hillsides surrounding it. You can walk down the boat ramp to the water's edge, but be careful of the broken glass. There are also trails leading up and around the hillside, and a stand of trees on the top for shade. There is also a turnout at the dam itself, and you can walk across to the other shore.
Of Note:	Two regular visitors informed me that the water had been rising for the past several weeks at this reservoir, so I trusted the ground at the edge. Otherwise, it's safer to climb up the hillside and be sure you are on stable ground.

Walk 8: Chesbro Reservoir

Location:	Oak Glen Avenue off Uvas Road—easy to find if you consult a map. See Map 23.
Parking:	Several turnouts
For Sports:	Usually boating and fishing, but boating has been discontinued during the drought
Description:	A reservoir impounded by an earthen dam and the surrounding hillsides. At present, the first several turnouts have NO TRESPASSING signs. What is usually the boat launch is gated and locked. You can still enter at the dam and get a look at how dismal our water situation is. There's still enough water to attract

herons, egrets and other waterfowl, though, and you may see red-tailed hawks and turkey buzzards soaring above you.

Of Note: At this and any other reservoir well below normal level, be careful about approaching the water's edge. What appears to be solid ground can in fact be a thin crust over a muddy quagmire. Dogs and people have been trapped in just this situation at Lexington Reservoir.

Walk 9: Anderson Reservoir

Location: Cochrane Road—easy to find if you consult a map. See Map 23.

Parking: Various lots

For Comfort: Restrooms, clean; water fountain

For Dining: 2 picnic areas

Description: The reservoir area itself was closed to the public on my visits, probably another result of the drought (or possibly encroaching contamination from United Technologies). But the picnic areas at the bottom of the hill were open. One area is in a wooded section along a stream; the second area is more open and sunny farther along the same stream. There are signs prohibiting swimming along most of the stream at the first picnic area, because of various intake and outflow pipes, but some areas which are not posted.

Of Note: A shady trail along the stream connects the two picnic areas. If you started from the far end of one area, walked to the far end of the second area, and returned to your start, it would be just over a mile. There is also a narrow trail leading up the hill onto the bank of the reservoir.

Walk 10: Coyote Lake

Location: Coyote Reservoir Road off Roop Road—hard to find, but signed. See Map 23.

Parking: At picnic area or campground

Description: Usually this is another in the chain of reservoirs, but it contained hardly any water at all on our visit. There's a pleasant picnic area in a large open meadow, and a nice campground amid small trees and open grassy areas. There are literally hundreds of ground squirrels, so be prepared for a high state of interest from your dog. There's lots of bird song and few people.

Of Note: Dogs are allowed only in day-use areas and the campground loop nearest the roadway, but that is still a good-sized area. The road in is very winding and not for the weak of stomach.

Dogs Are Not Welcome In

Santa Clara
Washington Park

Campbell
John D. Morgan Park
Campbell Park

Saratoga
Villa Montalvo
Hakone Gardens

Sunnyvale
Mango Park
Columbia Park
City section of Baylands

Cupertino
McClellan Ranch Park

Los Altos
Heritage Oaks Park
Lincoln Park
Marymeade Park
McKenzie Park
Shoup Park

Mountain View
Shoreline Park

Palo Alto
Foothills Park—on weekends

Santa Clara County
Ed R. Levin County Park
Calero Reservoir
Rancho San Antonio County Park
Sanborn Skyline County Park—except in picnic areas

Guadalupe Reservoir
Upper Stevens Creek County Park

Midpeninsula Regional Open Space Preserves
Monte Bello Open Space Preserve
Rancho San Antonio Open Space Preserve
Skyline Ridge Open Space Preserve
El Sereno Open Space Preserve
Sierra Azul Open Space Preserve
Saratoga Gap Open Space Preserve
Stevens Creek Nature Study Area

Part Three

San Mateo County

San Mateo is a county of only 530 square miles, and 77 of those are water. In the Bay Area, only the city and county of San Francisco is smaller. The cities tend to be more compact than in sprawling Santa Clara County. Many border either the bay or the ocean, and include beaches among their parks.

Dogs are not permitted in any San Mateo County parks. There are also three cities—San Carlos, Redwood City and San Bruno—which do not allow dogs in parks within their jurisdictions. However, San Bruno has converted a disused schoolyard into a dog exercise area, and San Carlos city managers are discussing creation of a dog park in the hills at the edge of their city. Redwood City currently has no plans to accommodate dog owners living there.

Portola Valley has no public parks, but it has a policy of not allowing dogs on trails within the township. Pacifica tends in the opposite direction, and has no leash law, but the county has an ordinance prohibiting dogs from running loose, so it's a moot point. Otherwise, all cities either currently have or are implementing leash and pooper-scooper laws. It can be difficult to comply with clean-up laws if you've walked to the far end of a beach and the nearest garbage can seems a mile away in the parking lot. Carry some sandwich bags and you can bag your dog's deposit and dispose of it when you leave.

The award for most parks per square mile in San Mateo County surely belongs to Foster City. Many include water, and canals are a major feature of Foster City. Your dog has to be on leash, but you're both allowed to wade or swim, so a visit here can be an interesting experience.

Chapter 1
Menlo Park and Atherton

Both cities have leash and cleanup regulations. Atherton has only one public park, but it's a beauty, well worth a visit. Most of Menlo's parks seem to be designed for specific sporting purposes and have only scattered areas of open grass. Burgess offers more room to roam, but the real winner as far as open space goes is the Baylands. Here you can wander over windswept hills or along the water's edge, shifting from one loop to another or making a straight journey parallel to the Bayfront Expressway.

Walk 1: Sharon Park

Location: Sharon Park Drive off Sand Hill Road—easy to find. See Map 24.

Size: 10 acres, all open

Parking: Limited street parking on side streets, not Sharon Park

Description: Rolling green lawn climbing up hill in front of huge housing complex. Paved path running through. Good shade areas. Attractive landscaping.

Of Note: Although 10 acres sounds like a large park, this is really a long narrow green space that runs in front of the housing development, and is probably meant more for the people who live here than anyone else.

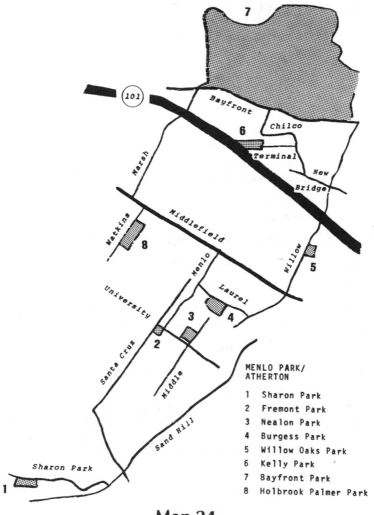

7

101

Bayfront

Chilco

6

Terminal

New

Bridge

Marsh

Middlefield

Watkins

8

Willow

5

Menlo

University

Laurel

4

3

2

Santa Cruz

Middle

MENLO PARK/
ATHERTON

1 Sharon Park
2 Fremont Park
3 Nealon Park
4 Burgess Park
5 Willow Oaks Park
6 Kelly Park
7 Bayfront Park
8 Holbrook Palmer Park

Sand Hill

Sharon Park

1

Map 24

Walk 2: Fremont Park

Location: University Drive and Santa Cruz Avenue—easy to
find. See Map 24.

Size: 0.8 acre, all open

Parking: Difficult—use the lots across University

Description: Small, flat park with very nice grass and enough large trees to shade nearly the entire park. Paved path meandering around.

Of Note: A very small but very attractive park. If it's not too hot and you have business downtown, you can take your dog for a stroll here before and after, leaving him in the car. But only if it's quite cool, of course.

Walk 3: Nealon Park

Location: Middle Avenue off El Camino Real—easy to find. See Map 24.

Size: 9 acres, about one-quarter open grass

Parking: Lots on and off Middle

For Comfort: Water fountain

For Sports: Practice putting green, fitness cluster, 5 tennis courts, fenced lighted softball field with bleachers

For Dining: 4 picnic tables

For Kids: Large playground, bike racks

Description: Flat, with good grass, what there is of it. Only small, separated, open areas offer grass, or in some cases, dirt and pine needles. Good shade around playground. Softball field fenced off. Nursery school fenced off. Large Little House Senior Center.

Of Note: This park seems to be dedicated to a lot of specific uses rather than an open green area. There were golf and tennis lessons going on while I was there.

Walk 4: Burgess Park

Location: Laurel Street and Burgess Drive—easy to find. See Map 24.

Size: 32 acres, about three-quarters open

Parking: Lot off Laurel, lot on Alma

For Comfort:	Water fountains
For Sports:	2 lighted tennis courts, sand volleyball court, swimming pool and swim center, fitness course, 2 softball fields with bleachers, soccer field
For Dining:	8 picnic tables, 1 barbecue; 1 group area
For Kids:	Playground, bike racks
Description:	Mostly flat except for a few small hills. Good grass. Paved, lighted path curving from lot on Laurel to Civic Center area. Nice areas of shade. Unfenced. Occasional train noise.
Of Note:	This park is next to the Civic Center, which also has acres of lush lawn and paved paths.

Walk 5: Willow Oaks Park

Location:	Willow Road and Coleman Avenue—easy to find. See Map 24.
Size:	2.5 acres, about two-thirds open grass
Parking:	Lot off Willow
For Comfort:	Restrooms, clean; water fountain
For Sports:	4 lighted tennis courts
For Dining:	1 picnic table

For Kids: Large playground

Description: Rolling terrain, with grass browning a bit. Good patches of shade, with two particularly huge old trees. Paved path makes big loop through park to Pope Street and Shirley Way.

Of Note: This park is close to two busy roads, but hills at the front buffer most of the traffic noise.

Walk 6: Kelly Park

Location: Terminal Avenue off Chilco Street—a little hard to find. See Map 24.

Size: 8.5 acres, very little open grass

Parking: Lot at end of Terminal

For Comfort: Restrooms, clean; water fountain

For Sports: 2 lighted tennis courts, swimming pool, fenced soccer/softball field

For Dining: 3 picnic tables, 3 barbecues

For Kids: Playground

Description: Flat, with all sorts of buildings and paths. The only real grass area is the playing field. Shade along one side of the field.

Of Note: The playing field is really the only open space in this park.

Walk 7: Bayfront Park

Location: Bayfront Expwy. just off Marsh Road—a little hard to find. See Map 24.

Size: 160 acres, all open

Parking: Several lots along access road

Description: Huge open space, with natural hills (except for the gazania planted all over one) surrounded by bay waters. This large peninsula is crisscrossed with both gravel and dirt trails, running around and up and over the hills and along the water. Hardly any shade. No drinking water. Can be sunny and hot. Trails lead on down along the bayfront toward Palo Alto and up toward Foster City. Egrets, pipits and other water-birds everywhere.

Of Note: You can really get in some hiking here. At lunchtime you're joined by walkers and runners from many of the businesses across Bayfront.

Walk 8: Holbrook Palmer Park

Location: Watkins Avenue off Middlefield Road —easy to find. See Map 24.

Size: Approximately 20 acres

Parking: Several lots, all entered by one access road off Watkins

For Comfort: Restrooms, very clean; water fountains

For Sports: 3 tennis courts

For Dining: 5 picnic tables scattered in the shade

For Kids: Playground

Description: Slightly rolling terrain. Large natural meadow at one end, rest very attractively planted. Big old trees for shade around much of park. Gravel paths winding everywhere. Main house contains park offices and community rooms where yoga lessons and such are given. Smaller building has gardening activities. Jennings Pavilion is a for-rent community building, with shaded courtyard.

Of Note: This is Atherton's only park, and it's a beauty. It was part of a gorgeous estate, and the buildings are still standing and still in use. The bird song is incredible.

Chapter 2
Belmont

A pleasant city with many fine homes, Belmont is also home to the combined expanse of Waterdog Park and John S. Brooks Memorial Open Space. Together they cover nearly a hundred acres. The path through them is wide, and even if you travel in the uphill direction, the slope is gentle.

Belmont has the usual leash and pooper-scooper laws. Unless you're on the flats near the bay, Belmont is a hilly city, so be sure your brakes are in good order and curb your wheels when you park.

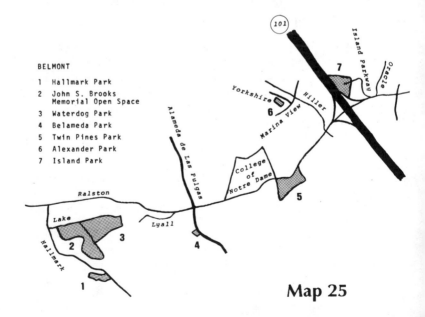

BELMONT

1   Hallmark Park
2   John S. Brooks
    Memorial Open Space
3   Waterdog Park
4   Belameda Park
5   Twin Pines Park
6   Alexander Park
7   Island Park

Map 25

Walk 1: Hallmark Park

Location: Hallmark Drive off Ralston Avenue—easy to find. See Map 25.

Size: 2.7 acres, mostly planted

Parking: Neighborhood street parking

For Comfort: Water fountain, pay phone

For Sports: 2 tennis courts

Description: Hillside mostly planted in small trees, hibiscus and ground cover. Few small grass areas. Paved path leads through, with a couple of benches placed so you can enjoy the fine view of San Francisco, the airport and the San Mateo Bridge. Quite windy, but very quiet. Not much shade.

Of Note: As you approach from Ralston, you can see an open-looking hillside on the right, which is the park. It abuts the large natural Fish and Game area, where dogs are not allowed.

Walk 2: John S. Brooks Memorial Open Space

Location: Lake Road off Hallmark Drive—easy to find. See Map 25.

Size: 49 acres, all natural

Parking: Neighborhood street parking

Description: A natural ravine, with houses above you on the hill-tops on both sides. An old dirt road leads steadily down along one side of the ravine. A narrow trail leads off to the right, down into the ravine and up the other side. A tiny creek sometimes runs beside the road for a short distance, providing a drink for your dog. It's hard to tell when you leave the Open Space and enter Waterdog Park (not that it matters), but when you reach the lake, you know you're in Waterdog. You can continue on through Waterdog and come out on Lyall

Way at the other end, a total of about 1½ miles one way.

Of Note: If you come in the spring, the hillsides are colorful with wildflowers. You can find lupine, poppies, odd-looking Indian paintbrush and other charming flowers.

Walk 3: Waterdog Lake Park

Location: Through John S. Brooks Memorial Open Space or via trail from Lyall Way—a bit hard to find and to reach. See Map 25.

Size: 50 acres, all natural

Parking: Neighborhood street parking at both ends

For Sports: Fishing (but no boating, swimming or wading)

Description: This is an open natural ravine and hillsides, which lead into the John S. Brooks Memorial Open Space, continues as a narrower trail, and enters the San Francisco Watershed (where you and your dog must stop, as dogs are not allowed). From Lyall Way, take the old gravel road up a hill past apartments and houses, then drop under arching oaks. You will reach Waterdog Lake in about ¾ mile, with a side road leading down to the dam. Continue on and at some unknown point you will cross into the Brooks Open Space. A total of about 1½ miles will bring you out on Lake Road. You can continue across the street on a narrower, steeper trail for ½ mile.

Of Note: You are never far from civilization, with houses lining the tops of the canyon on both sides, but it's quiet, there are all kinds of wildlife, and the trail winds from sun to shade. The grade is gentle, and even though it's uphill nearly all the way from Lyall, it's not a hard climb.

Walk 4: Belameda Park

Location:	Alameda de Las Pulgas near Ralston Avenue—easy to find. See Map 25.
Size:	3 acres, about two-thirds open
Parking:	Lot off Alameda de Las Pulgas
For Comfort:	Water fountain
For Dining:	3 picnic tables, 3 barbecues
For Kids:	Playground, bike racks
Description:	Park is stepped into the hillside, with some small flat patches of lawn. Paved paths carve the park into several little areas. Mostly sun, but a couple of nicely shaded areas. Traffic noise from Alameda de Las Pulgas.
Of Note:	This park is next to the library, so you can combine some reading with an outing for your dog.

Walk 5: Twin Pines Park

Location:	Ralston Avenue near College of Notre Dame—easy to find. See Map 25.
Size:	8 acres developed plus open space
Parking:	4-hour parking on Ralston, and lot off Ralston
For Comfort:	Restrooms, clean, wheelchair access; water fountains; pay phone
For Sports:	Horseshoe pits in group picnic area
For Dining:	8 picnic tables, 2 barbecues; 1 group picnic area
For Kids:	Playground
Description:	Slightly sloping ground, mostly wooded. Paved path runs through. Quiet stream in gully, with bridge leading to group picnic area and some open space. Fenced. Surprisingly little traffic noise from Ralston. Mostly shaded.
Of Note:	This would be a nice cool park for a sunny day.

Walk 6: Alexander Park

Location: Access from Yorkshire Way—hard to find. See Map 25.

Size: 1.3 acres, about three-quarters open

Parking: Neighborhood street parking

For Comfort: Primitive restroom, barely functioning water fountain

For Sports: 3 tennis courts

For Dining: 2 picnic tables, 2 barbecues

For Kids: Large playground

Description: Fairly flat, with nice grass, what there is of it. Not much shade. Paved path across width. Mostly fenced.

Of Note: This is a smallish park and hard to find if you aren't familiar with the area. There's just a drive leading in from Yorkshire. But if you happen to live nearby, it's bigger than your lawn.

Walk 7: Island Park

Location: Oracle Drive on left off Ralston Avenue—a little hard to find the right access road. See Map 25.

Size: 12.5 acres, all open or softball fields

Parking: Several lots

For Comfort: Restrooms, clean, wheelchair access; water fountain

For Sports: Lighted softball fields

Description: The entire area is under construction, and it's difficult to tell what the final product will be like. Right now the best place for dog walkers is a path along the slough past the farthest ball field.

Of Note: If the chaos is too much for you here, there are paved paths around all the lagoons in the huge business complex running along this stretch of Ralston. At lunchtime, they are heavily used by office workers, but at other times you can have a nice sunny stroll.

Chapter 3
Foster City

This is an unusual little city, isolated on an isthmus, with canals everywhere around and through it. Once you find your way in, running into a park is almost inevitable—Foster City seems to have them everywhere. Several of them lie along some of the many canals, and swimming *is* allowed. You can also connect with a portion of the Bay Trail here, a sunny paved ramble along the bay.

Foster City has leash and pooper-scooper laws. Finding your way in and out of the city can be a challenge if you don't consult a map. Once you're there, the roads mostly run in circles.

Comfort amenities, such as restrooms and water fountains, don't seem to be an important feature of Foster City parks, so you might want to acquaint yourself with where these can be found in case you need one. Picnic tables are also fairly scarce.

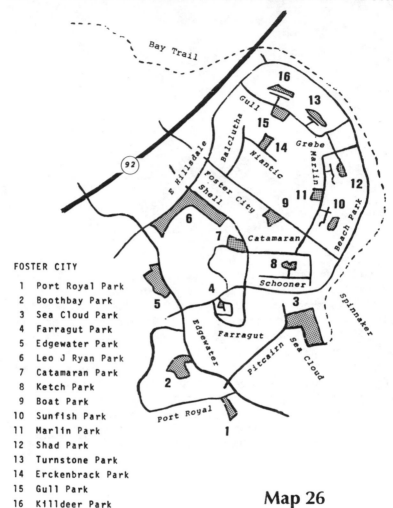

FOSTER CITY

1   Port Royal Park
2   Boothbay Park
3   Sea Cloud Park
4   Farragut Park
5   Edgewater Park
6   Leo J Ryan Park
7   Catamaran Park
8   Ketch Park
9   Boat Park
10 Sunfish Park
11 Marlin Park
12 Shad Park
13 Turnstone Park
14 Erckenbrack Park
15 Gull Park
16 Killdeer Park

Map 26

Walk 1: Port Royal Park

Location: Port Royal Avenue off Edgewater Blvd.—easy to find. See Map 26.

Size: 4 acres, all open space

Parking: Lot off Port Royal

For Comfort: Portable toilet; water fountain

For Sports: Soccer field

For Dining:	3 picnic tables
For Kids:	Playground
Description:	Seems to be a fairly new park. Flat, with nice grass. Trees are very young and do not offer any shade. Path along one side, with benches.
Of Note:	This will probably be a more attractive park when the plantings have had time to mature. For now, it's a great place in cool weather when you want lots of sun.

Walk 2: Boothbay Park

Location:	Edgewater Blvd. and Boothbay Avenue—easy to find. See Map 26.
Size:	11.2 acres, about three-quarters open
Parking:	Lot off Galveston
For Comfort:	Portable toilet; water fountain
For Sports:	4 tennis courts, basketball court, 2 softball fields
For Dining:	6 picnic tables, 4 barbecues
For Kids:	Playground
Description:	Rolling terrain with nice grass. Paved path winds across between opposite corners. A few small, pleasant areas of shade. Unfenced.
Of Note:	This appears to be the only park in Foster City that provides barbecues along with picnic tables (which are also relatively scarce).

Walk 3: Sea Cloud Park

Location:	Pitcairn Drive and Sea Cloud Court—a little hard to find. See Map 26.
Size:	26 acres, nearly all open
Parking:	Lot off Pitcairn, lot at end of Sea Cloud
For Comfort:	Restrooms, clean; water fountain

For Sports: 3 fenced baseball fields, soccer field, football field

For Dining: 6 picnic tables scattered in odd corners

Description: Mostly flat, with nice lush grass. Good patches of shade. Paved, lighted path running down length and across width. Mostly enclosed by water.

Of Note: This is a big L-shaped park, and a walk around it with a stop for a swim at the rubbly beach loaded with ducks is quite an outing.

Walk 4: Farragut Park

Location: Farragut and Beach Park blvds.—easy to find. See Map 26.

Size: 3.8 acres, all open space

Parking: Neighborhood street parking

For Kids: Playground

Description: This is really just a large open field, fairly flat, with a playground stuck on one end. There are no trees and hence no shade.

Of Note: If you like sun and grass, this is probably the place for you.

Walk 5: Edgewater Park

Location: Polaris Avenue or Edgewater Blvd.—easy to find. See Map 26.

Size: 8.6 acres, mostly open

Parking: Street on Polaris, small lot along Edgewater

For Comfort: Portable toilet; water fountain

For Sports: Lighted softball field, 2 tennis courts, basketball court

For Kids: Playground

Description: Slightly rolling, with weedy grass but lots of it. Paved path through and along one side of park. Unfenced. Some nice shade trees.

Of Note: One of the larger of the nonbeach parks, with a pleasing proportion of sun and shade. Bees seem to be attracted to the variety of weeds mixed with the grass, so use some caution if you plan to sit or walk barefoot.

Walk 6: Leo J. Ryan Memorial Park

Location: Shell and East Hillsdale blvds.—easy to find. See Map 26.

Size: 14.3 acres, about three-quarters open

Parking: Long lot off Shell

For Comfort: Restrooms, clean; water fountain

For Sports: Parcourse, 6 lighted tennis courts, basketball courts, boat launch, volleyball courts

For Dining: 5 picnic tables tucked in courtyard at corner of Recreation Building

Description: Fairly flat along Shell, hillier in the center. Flat again along Hillsdale. Paved path or boardwalk along the water. Paved path weaving through the entire park. Stepped amphitheater with very lush grass. The rest of the grass is somewhat sparse. Nice landscaping in most of park. Good patches of shade.

Of Note: This is one of Foster City's biggest parks, and its L-shape means you can have quite a nice walk around its perimeter. The Recreation Building offers such community services as meeting rooms, an auditorium, a kitchen, and ceramics and other arts and crafts rooms.

Walk 7: Catamaran Park

Location: Catamaran Street and Shell Blvd.—easy to find. See Map 26.

Size: 5.7 acres, nearly all open

Parking: Street on Catamaran

For Comfort: Portable toilet; water fountain

For Sports: 2 lighted tennis courts, basketball court, soccer field

For Kids: Playground

Description: Low ridge running through park, otherwise flat. Nice grass. Sand beach. Paved promenade along water. Limited shade.

Of Note: If your dog is agreeable to trying new things, you can climb onto the promenade from the beach and leave him below. Then, as you walk along the promenade, he swims below and alongside you (or, if he's as big as my dog, walks on his tiptoes most of the way).

Walk 8: Ketch Park

Location: Topsail Court—a little hard to find. See Map 26.

Size: 1.6 acres, nearly all open

Parking: Neighborhood street parking

For Sports: Basketball courts

For Kids: Playground

Description: Flat and open, with acceptable grass. Paved path through. Not much shade, and seems even smaller than it is.

Of Note: Not worth taking the trouble to find unless you happen to live nearby.

Walk 9: Boat Park

Location:	Foster City Blvd. and Bounty Drive—easy to find. See Map 26.
Size:	3.2 acres, nearly all parking lot
Parking:	Large lot off Foster City Blvd.
For Sports:	Boat launch
For Dining:	2 picnic tables
Description:	Mostly a paved parking lot. Short boardwalk along one of the canals. Tables in the full sun alongside the water.
Of Note:	This is not a very inviting place. Although picnic facilities are scarce in Foster City parks, there are other places more appealing than this.

Walk 10: Sunfish Park

Location:	Access off Sunfish Court, Mullet Court or Halibut Street—look for drive between houses. See Map 26.
Size:	2.4 acres, nearly all open
Parking:	Neighborhood street parking
For Sports:	Basketball courts
For Kids:	Playground
Description:	Rolling, with grass somewhat weedy. Lighted, paved path down length, with benches spaced along it. Not much shade. Fenced.
Of Note:	One of several small parks completely surrounded by houses, this is the most square of the bunch, rather than long and narrow. It seems smaller because of the shape.

Walk 11: Marlin Park

Location: Marlin Avenue—easy to find. See Map 26.

Size: 3.1 acres, all open space

Parking: Neighborhood street parking

For Comfort: Restrooms: the men's was unlocked but the women's was locked

For Kids: Playground

Description: Slightly rolling, with nice grass area. Good landscaping and large shade trees. Paved path runs around park and leads down to sand beach.

Of Note: Another park where swimming is allowed, and a nice sand beach with gradual dropoff.

Walk 12: Shad Park

Location: Access from Shad Court, Grebe Street, Bluefish Court or Tarpon Street—look for drive between houses. See Map 26.

Size: 2.1 acres, nearly all open

Parking: Neighborhood street parking

For Sports: Basketball courts

For Kids: Playground

Description: Rolling with small hills. Grass sparse and weedy. Long, narrow area. Lighted, paved path down length. Not much shade. Fenced. Lots of kids in the playground.

Of Note: One of the smallest of the Foster City neighborhood parks.

Walk 13: Turnstone Park

Location: Access from Turnstone Court, Avocet Court, Grebe Street or Loon Court—look for the drive between houses. See Map 26.

Size:	1.5 acres, nearly all open
Parking:	Neighborhood street parking
For Sports:	Basketball courts
For Kids:	Playground
Description:	Slightly rolling, with lush grass. Long and narrow with lighted, paved path down length. Patches of landscaping. Benches along path. Areas of shade. Fenced. Quiet.
Of Note:	Unfortunately there is a sewer access in the park and you can smell the sewage flowing beneath you.

Walk 14: Erckenbrack Park

Location:	Niantic Drive—a little hard to find. See Map 26.
Size:	3.5 acres, nearly all open
Parking:	Small lot off Niantic
For Comfort:	Restroom building barred and in state of slow collapse; filthy portable toilet
For Kids:	Playground
Description:	Fairly flat, with scrubby grass. Several decent patches of shade. Goes down to another sand beach, with ducks, geese and gulls.
Of Note:	Swimming is allowed. This is more in a neighborhood than some of the other beach parks, and it seems to receive more use.

Walk 15: Gull Park

Location:	Gull Avenue—easy to find. See Map 26.
Size:	3.1 acres, all open space
Parking:	Neighborhood street parking
For Comfort:	Restrooms (locked)
For Kids:	Playground

Description: Slightly rolling, with very nice grass. Some good shade trees scattered in the park. Paved path around. Airplane noise overhead. Curved sand beach.

Of Note: Swimming is allowed at the beach, and you and your dog can go in together. The dropoff is mostly quite gradual. There are ducks and gulls in abundance.

Walk 16: Killdeer Park

Location: Access from Killdeer Court, Sandpiper Court or Stilt Court—look for the driveway between houses. See Map 26.

Size: 2.4 acres, all open space

Parking: Neighborhood street parking

For Kids: Playground

Description: Mostly flat, with good grass. Long, narrow park with lighted, paved path running down the length, and benches scattered along it. Areas of landscaping. Some shade. Fenced. Quiet.

Of Note: Another of the small parks completely surrounded by houses. Unless you lived in the neighborhood, you'd never know these secluded parks existed.

Walk 17: Bay Trail (Foster City section)

Location: Access off East Hillsdale Blvd. (turn in at sign for fishing pier). See Map 26.

Parking: Dirt lot for San Mateo County fishing pier

Description: Paved, wide trail for bicyclists and pedestrians. Mostly flat, completely in the sun except where it passes under the San Mateo Bridge. Runs from north edge of Foster City to south edge. Rough rock scramble separates the path from the bay. Lots of waterbirds, including egrets.

Of Note: You could really fry your brains on a hot summer day, but when the fog is in or the weather is cooler, this is a beauty.

Chapter 4
San Mateo

San Mateo is a sprawling sort of city, well endowed with parks. About half are smallish, the other half large enough for a good romp—one is over 200 acres. Dogs are welcome in all the city parks, but not the county's Coyote Point. This prohibition forces an abrupt stop for dog walkers on the Bay Trail, but you can start from the edge of Coyote Point and walk all the way through San Mateo and Foster City, so it's not much of an inconvenience.

The usual leash and clean-up laws apply.

Walk 1: Laurelwood Park

Location:	De Anza Blvd.—easy to find. See Map 27.
Size:	225.3 acres, all open space
Parking:	Neighborhood street parking
For Comfort:	Water fountain
For Dining:	3 picnic tables
For Kids:	Playground
Description:	Two large natural hills and the valley between them. Paved road closed to vehicles runs down steeply at first, then gradually as you progress through the park, finally up and over a boundary hill before exiting on the other side. Dirt trails run steeply up the hill on one side. Another dirt trail runs along the flank of the hill on the other side. There is a large open meadow where you first enter the park.
Of Note:	A lively little stream runs along the valley, and is accessible in places. There are all kinds of frogs, birds and rabbits.

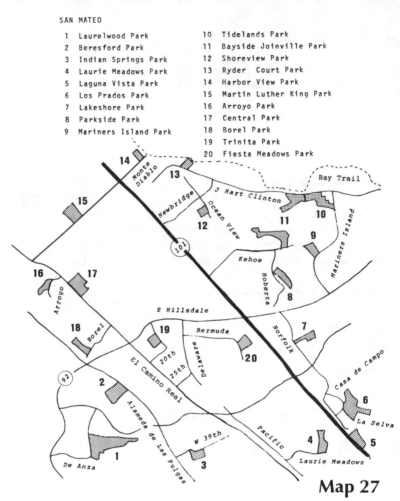

SAN MATEO

1   Laurelwood Park
2   Beresford Park
3   Indian Springs Park
4   Laurie Meadows Park
5   Laguna Vista Park
6   Los Prados Park
7   Lakeshore Park
8   Parkside Park
9   Mariners Island Park
10 Tidelands Park
11 Bayside Joinville Park
12 Shoreview Park
13 Ryder Court Park
14 Harbor View Park
15 Martin Luther King Park
16 Arroyo Park
17 Central Park
18 Borel Park
19 Trinita Park
20 Fiesta Meadows Park

Map 27

Walk 2: Beresford Park

Location: Alameda de Las Pulgas—easy to find. See Map 27.

Size: 18.5 acres, about half open area

Parking: Lots off Parkside and Alameda de Las Pulgas

For Comfort: Restrooms, with wheelchair access, clean; water fountains

For Sports: 4 lighted tennis courts, basketball/handball courts, 3 lighted fenced softball fields

For Dining: 18 picnic tables, 9 barbecues, plus group area under shade arbor

For Kids: Large playground

Description: Partly flat, partly slightly sloping ground with lush grass. Not a lot of shade. Paved, lighted path runs along two sides of field and on through park. Sunny lawn area. Well used. Recreation building has dance and other programs.

Of Note: The San Mateo Garden Center has one section of the grounds beautifully landscaped.

Walk 3: Indian Springs Park

Location: West 39th Avenue off Hacienda Street—easy to find. See Map 27.

Size: 2.7 acres, all open

Parking: Lot on West 39th

For Comfort: Restroom building, but padlocked

For Dining: 2 picnic tables, 1 barbecue

For Kids: Small playground

Description: Cut into a hillside, with central flat area and rest sloping. Mostly natural terrain under old eucalyptus trees. Little drainage ditches are seeping everywhere, possibly evidence of the springs for which it is named. Shady and quiet, but lots of garbage thrown around the picnic tables.

Of Note: This park was not all that attractive from a human perspective, but my dog seemed to find it quite fascinating.

Walk 4: Laurie Meadows Park

Location: Laurie Meadows Drive—a little hard to find. See Map 27.

Size: 5.3 acres, nearly all open

Parking: Unknown at this time

Description: At the present, this park is closed while being renovated. It looks as if it will be a very nice park, with a path around the perimeter, a playground, and possibly other facilities.

Of Note: If you're interested in visiting here, you might want to check with San Mateo Parks and Recreation first.

Walk 5: Laguna Vista Park

Location: Apartment complex off La Selva—follow the signs for the Bayfront Bike Path. See Map 27.

Size: 2 acres, all open

Parking: Visitor parking in apartment complex (limited)

Description: This is really what the signs say, a bike path, more than a park. But if you can find a place to park, it provides access to a paved path running around Marina Lagoon, and can provide a nice walk or jog, or even a bike ride for you and your dog (presumably the dog won't be riding the bike, but who knows).

Of Note: Since this is entirely in the sun, it would be a good walk for a cool day. It's certainly less used than the popular Bay Trail along the bay.

Walk 6: Los Prados Park

Location: Casa de Campo off La Selva—a little hard to find. See Map 27.

Size: 12.6 acres, nearly all open space

Parking: Lot off Casa de Campo

For Comfort: Restrooms, clean, but no doors on stalls; water fountain currently not working right

For Sports: 2 soccer fields, softball field, parcourse, 2 lighted tennis courts, lighted basketball court

For Dining: 3 picnic tables

For Kids: Playground

Description: Fairly flat, with nice grass. Mostly sunny, with a few small pockets of shade. Paved path around perimeter. Unfenced. Quiet.

Of Note: The irregular shape makes an interesting walk around the edge of the park.

Walk 7: Lakeshore Park

Location: Marina Court off Norfolk Street—easy to find. See Map 27.

Size: 4.2 acres, all open

Parking: Lot on Marina

For Comfort: Restrooms, water fountain in recreation building

For Sports: 2 softball fields, basketball courts

For Dining: 5 picnic tables, 2 barbecues

For Kids: Playground

Description: Flat, with grass only on the playing fields. Fields separately fenced. Nice wide sand beach with gentle slope into water.

Of Note: This park is a water dog's dream come true. Humans are allowed to wade and dogs can swim, and there are even schools of tiny fish darting about in the shallows, which are lots of fun to chase.

Walk 8: Parkside Aquatic Park

Location: Seal Street off Roberta Drive—easy to find. See Map 27.

Size: 3.4 acres, nearly all open

Parking: Lot off Seal

For Comfort: Water fountain

For Dining: 5 picnic tables, 4 barbecues

Description: Fairly flat grass strip along Marina Lagoon. Lighted, paved path with benches runs along top of canal side. Nearly all sun.

Of Note: Redevelopment was going on during my visit, so things could change here. At present, it's mostly a place to sit and watch the water or have a sunny picnic.

Walk 9: Mariners Island Park

Location: Mariners Island Blvd.—easy to find. See Map 27.

Size: 4 acres, all open

Parking: Neighborhood street parking

For Sports: Softball field, parcourse

For Kids: Playground

Description: Slightly rolling, with lush grass. Paved, lighted path around. Mostly sun, with one small area of shade. Lagoon runs along one side. Quiet and attractive.

Of Note: The water is accessible and deep enough for a large dog on a 6-foot leash to swim while you walk along the bank.

Walk 10: Tidelands Park

Location: J. Hart Clinton Drive and Mariners Island Blvd.—easy to find. See Map 27.

Size: 10.9 acres, all open

Parking: Neighborhood street parking

Description: Mostly flat, scrubby natural area under high powerlines. Path continues from Bayside Joinville Park along the lagoon. Sunny.

Of Note: This does not yet qualify as a park, only as an open area. There may be plans for development. If you are interested, contact the San Mateo Parks and Recreation Department.

Walk 11: Bayside Joinville Park

Location: Kehoe Avenue—easy to find. See Map 27.

Size: 20.5 acres, nearly all open

Parking: Lot off Kehoe

For Comfort: Restrooms, with wheelchair access, clean; water fountains

For Sports: 2 lighted tennis courts, lighted softball field, horseshoe pits, swimming pool

For Dining: 4 small game/picnic tables; group area with 18 picnic tables and 2 large barbecues

For Kids: Playground

Description: Actually two sections of park connected by a pedestrian bridge over the lagoon. Fairly flat, with nice grass. Some shade but mostly sun. Attractive landscaping. Paved path loops around both sections. Quiet. Waterfowl on the canal and a small island in the lagoon.

Of Note: You can get to the water on the far side of the lagoon, although accomplishing this without trampling the landscaping or letting your dog off leash is quite a feat.

Walk 12: Shoreview Park

Location: Ocean View Avenue near Cottage Grove Avenue—a little hard to find. See Map 27.

Size: 4.8 acres, about one-third open

Parking: Lot off Ocean View

For Comfort: Restrooms and fountain in community building

For Sports: 2 lighted tennis courts, softball field

For Dining: 2 individual picnic tables, plus group area with 4 tables and 2 barbecues

For Kids: Playground

Description: Mostly flat, with nice grass. Entire park fenced. Field fenced off separately. Paved path around community building, dirt path along playground and open area. Lots of shade. Quiet.

Of Note: There's not a lot of open space here, but what there is is mostly shaded.

Walk 13: Ryder Court Park

Location: End of Ryder Street—hard to find—off J. Hart Clinton Drive—easy to find. See Map 27.

Size: 2.1 acres, all open

Parking: Neighborhood street parking, or lot off J. Hart Clinton

For Dining: 1 picnic table, 1 barbecue

For Kids: Playground

Description: Slightly rolling, with lush grass. Nice big areas of shade. Unfenced. Quiet.

Of Note: Another spot to gain access to the Bay Trail, or, if you started somewhere else, to rest in the shade after all the sun on the trail.

Walk 14: Harbor View Park

Location: Monte Diablo Avenue off Bayshore Blvd.—a little hard to find. See Map 27.

Size: 2.5 acres, all open

Parking: Neighborhood street parking

For Sports: Softball field

For Dining: 4 picnic tables under building overhang

For Kids: Playground

Description: Flat, with good grass. Most of the grass area is actually the playing field. Fenced. Quiet except for planes overhead.

Of Note: This is a good place to picnic and get out of the sun if you've been walking the sunny Bay Trail.

Walk 15: Martin Luther King Jr. Park

Location: East Santa Inez Avenue at North Fremont Street— easy to find. See Map 27.

Size: 6.1 acres, about three-quarters open space

Parking: Neighborhood street parking

For Comfort: Restrooms open when pool is open

For Sports: Lighted softball field/soccer field, basketball courts, swimming pool

For Dining: 9 picnic tables, 2 barbecues

For Kids: Playground

Description: Flat, big lawn area with trees around the edges for shade. Fenced. Small separately fenced garden area. Paved path across park.

Of Note: I encountered several people with their dogs running loose, so be aware.

Walk 16: Arroyo Court Park

Location: Arroyo Court—a little hard to find—off El Camino Real. See Map 27.

Size: 1.4 acres, all open

Parking: Neighborhood street parking

Description: The site of a camp of the De Anza expedition. They chose a lovely, shady creekside location. Steps lead down to a wide embankment with benches along a sluggish stream. Farther along the stream, a rough dirt trail leads along and down to a faster, cleaner section of the stream, with access to the water. There's lots of bird song.

Of Note: There's a hole with water deep enough to force even my large Newfoundland mix to swim.

Walk 17: Central Park

Location: 5th Avenue and El Camino Real—easy to find. See Map 27.

Size: 16.3 acres, nearly all open

Parking: Metered street parking on Laurel, limited free street parking on 9th

For Sports: Lighted softball field, 6 lighted tennis courts

For Dining: Large group area with tables and barbecues

For Kids: Playground, miniature railroad

Description: Mostly flat, with lush grass. Paved paths snaking everywhere. Lots of planted areas, and plenty of ID tags on plants. Many good areas of shade. Quiet. Dogs not allowed in the Japanese Garden section of the park.

Of Note: If you approach from 9th Avenue, you head directly toward a large statue of a dog, realistic enough to make my own large dog cautious until he identified it as a fake. There is no explanation of why it is there.

Walk 18: Borel Park

Location:	Shafter Street at Borel Avenue—easy to find. See Map 27.
Size:	1.6 acres, all open
Parking:	Neighborhood street parking
Description:	This is really just a weedy vacant lot with some eucalyptus trees, certainly not worth a visit.

Walk 19: Trinita Park

Location:	19th Avenue—a little hard to find. See Map 27.
Size:	2 acres, all open
Parking:	Neighborhood street parking
For Sports:	2 softball fields, basketball court
For Comfort:	Restrooms, clean; water fountain
For Kids:	Playground
Description:	Mostly flat, well-kept fields, with a dirt path around and between them. Each field is separately fenced, and the whole park is mostly fenced. No shade. Some traffic noise from 92.
Of Note:	This is mostly the 2 softball fields and a playground.

Walk 20: Fiesta Meadows Park

Location:	Bermuda Drive off Delaware Street—this is the *only* way in. See Map 27.
Size:	4.7 acres, all open
Parking:	Lot off Bermuda
For Sports:	Softball field
Description:	A large open grass field, all in the sun. This is a convenient place for a romp if you happen to live nearby, but certainly not worth the trouble to find otherwise.
Of Note:	A new swim club is apparently being built here, so further plans may be in the works for this one.

Chapter 5
Burlingame

Burlingame has a pleasant scattering of parks throughout the city. Most are rather small, but there are two exceptions: Washington Park is large and civilized, cool and green and shady. Mill Canyon Open Space is large and uncivilized, with a rough narrow trail and a slope that is in places severe. If you want to be alone, Mill Canyon is a good choice, but you might also be able to find some more civilized solitude in Bayside Park, as long as no softball is being played.

Burlingame has the usual leash and clean-up laws. Traffic around the frontage roads can be hectic, so be sure you know where you're going before you set out.

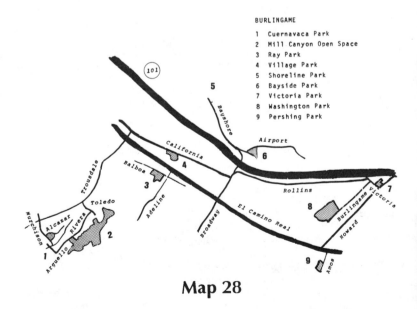

BURLINGAME

1 Cuernavaca Park
2 Mill Canyon Open Space
3 Ray Park
4 Village Park
5 Shoreline Park
6 Bayside Park
7 Victoria Park
8 Washington Park
9 Pershing Park

Map 28

Walk 1: Cuernavaca Park

Location:	Hunt Drive at Alcazar Drive—a little hard to find. See Map 28.
Size:	5 acres, about half open grass
Parking:	Lot off Alcazar
For Comfort:	Restrooms, clean; water fountain
For Sports:	Baseball field with bleachers, basketball court
For Dining:	5 picnic tables under shade gazebo
For Kids:	Playground
Description:	Slightly rolling areas on different plateaus connected by stairs. Field fenced off from rest of park. Not much shade except in picnic area. Paved at picnic area only. Unfenced. Quiet.
Of Note:	The upper tier of the park offers excellent views of the airport, including the runways. You can sit and watch planes take off and land.

Walk 2: Mill Canyon Open Space

Location:	Arguello Drive between Escalante Way and Sebastian Drive—easy to find if you're watching for it. See Map 28.
Size:	49 acres, all natural
Parking:	Neighborhood street parking
Description:	A ravine and most of the hills on both sides, with houses at the top. The trail is not very appealing at the start, but if you forge on to the left it plunges in amid trees and wildflowers. It's downhill or flat most of the way in, and can be pretty rough and muddy in places. Two uphill pulls on the return trip are steep enough to pick up your heart rate. Covers about ¾ mile one way.
Of Note:	There are survey markers along the trail, so perhaps there are plans for some improvement.

Walk 3: Ray Park

Location: Balboa Way at Devereaux Drive—easy to find. See Map 28.

Size: 5.9 acres, nearly all open

Parking: Lot off Balboa

For Comfort: Restrooms, clean; water fountain; pay phone

For Sports: 2 tennis courts, baseball field, basketball courts, handball court

For Kids: Playground

Description: Mostly flat, with large open field. Good shade mostly around playground. Natural area under trees. Completely fenced. Quiet.

Of Note: The field seems to become boggy quickly if it has rained recently, so come when it's been dry for a few days.

Walk 4: Village Park

Location: California Drive between Oxford Road and Rosedale Avenue—easy to find. See Map 28.

Size: 1.9 acres, about three-quarters open grass

Parking: Neighborhood street parking

For Comfort: Restrooms, clean; water fountain

For Sports: Basketball court

For Dining: 5 picnic tables

For Kids: Playground

Description: Flat, mostly lush grass. Paved path runs across width. Very little shade. Some traffic noise from California. Train also runs nearby. Completely fenced.

Of Note: In other towns this would be a small park; in Burlingame it's probably about average.

Walk 5: Shoreline Park

Location: Bayshore Highway between Mahler and Burlway roads—easy to find. See Map 28.

Size: 2.31 acres, all open

Parking: Very limited street parking

Description: A small inlet, with a walkway around it and a bridge across it, stuck in amid car-rental outlets and restaurants. There were no shorebirds of any kind there on my visit.

Of Note: It's almost impossible to park here, and there's not much of a walk once you do. If you want to walk along the water, go to Menlo Park's Bayfront Park.

Walk 6: Bayside Park

Location: Airport Blvd.—easy to find. See Map 28.

Size: 12 acres, about three-quarters open

Parking: Lot off Airport

For Comfort: Restrooms, clean; water fountain; pay phone

For Sports: 3 baseball fields, 1 with lights and bleachers; soccer field

For Kids: Playground

Description: Fairly flat, with good grass. Nice areas of shade. Paved path runs along two sides. A rubbly area at one end was of great interest to my dog. The lighted field is fenced, with a KEEP OFF sign. Lots of traffic noise from 101.

Of Note: This is not a place a lot of people seem to come to, since the area is mostly parking lots for the airport. The park is rarely crowded.

Walk 7: Victoria Park

Location: Howard Avenue at Victoria Road—easy to find. See
                     Map 28.

Size: 0.93 acres, about half open grass

Parking: Neighborhood street parking

For Comfort: Water fountain

For Sports: Basketball court

For Dining: 2 picnic tables

For Kids: Playground

Description: Flat, with nice grass. Good areas of shade. Fenced.
                     Quiet.

Of Note: Even for Burlingame, this is a small park.

Walk 8: Washington Park

Location: Carolan and Burlingame avenues—easy to find. See
                     Map 28.

Size: 18.90 acres, about seven-eighths open grass

Parking: Lots off Burlingame and Carolan

For Comfort: Restrooms, clean; water fountains; pay phone

For Sports: 4 lighted tennis courts, bocce courts, horseshoe pits, 2
                     lighted baseball fields with bleachers, basketball
                     courts

For Dining: 11 picnic tables, 6 barbecues

For Kids: Playground (under renovation on my visit)

Description: Fairly flat, with nice grass areas and huge old, gor-
                     geous trees for shade, particularly on side nearest El
                     Camino. Lighted, paved paths running everywhere
                     through the park. Lots of squirrels for entertainment.
                     Contains recreation center and senior center.

Of Note: This is the jewel of Burlingame's parks, so cool and
                     appealing with all the trees, yet with fine patches of
                     sunlit grass.

Walk 9: Pershing Park

Location: Crescent Avenue at Newlands Avenue—a little hard to find. See Map 28.

Size: 1.1 acres, less than half open grass

Parking: Neighborhood street parking

For Sports: Basketball court

For Dining: 3 small picnic tables

For Kids: Large playground

Description: A small hill, with the grass slightly parching. Paved path runs on a diagonal through the park. Attractive shade arbor over the tables and some benches. Lots of kids and parents.

Of Note: This park is in a nice residential area, and seems to be a meeting place for moms and kids.

Chapter 6
Millbrae

    Millbrae is a small city with small parks. Only Central Park offers an expanse of any size. The five other parks are useful mainly for anyone who lives nearby. If you happen to be an airplane buff, Mills Estate Park might interest you, with its excellent view straight down two of SFO's runways. Like most cities, Millbrae has leash and pooper-scooper laws.

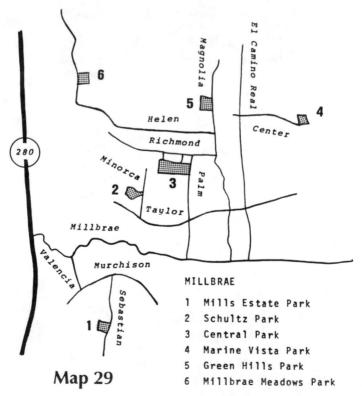

Map 29

MILLBRAE

1   Mills Estate Park
2   Schultz Park
3   Central Park
4   Marine Vista Park
5   Green Hills Park
6   Millbrae Meadows Park

Walk 1: Mills Estate Park

Location:	Sebastian Drive off Trousdale Drive—easy to find. See Map 29.
Size:	About 1.5 acres
Parking:	Neighborhood street parking
For Kids:	Playground
Description:	Flat grass area surrounded by seminatural hillsides. Beware of foxtails and other burrs. Mostly sun, with the only shade being on the hillsides. Paved path up one side to playground area. Quiet except for occasional airport noise.
Of Note:	From the meadow, you look directly down on two of San Francisco Airport's runways.

Walk 2: Schultz Park

Location:	Minorca Way off Hillcrest Blvd.—a little hard to find. See Map 29.
Size:	About 1 acre
Parking:	Neighborhood street parking
Description:	Short climb up paved path to small shady meadow surrounded by seminatural hillsides leading up to houses. Mostly fenced. Quiet except for some airport noise.
Of Note:	Minorca is a divided street; as you reach Taylor, you can see the sign for the park.

Walk 3: Central Park

Location:	Palm Avenue or Lincoln Circle—easy to find. See Map 29.
Size:	About 15 acres
Parking:	Street parking on Palm, lot off Lincoln
For Comfort:	Restrooms in recreation building; water fountain

For Sports:	Parcourse, 4 lighted tennis courts, lighted softball field, basketball court, recreation building
For Dining:	7 picnic tables
For Kids:	2 playgrounds
Description:	Rolling, with slightly browning grass. Lots of sun. but also good areas of shade. Paved path makes big loop around park. About half fenced. Lots of kids in playgrounds.
Of Note:	Millbrae's biggest park, and quite an attractive one.

Walk 4: Marine Vista Park

Location:	Bay Street off Center Street—hard to find. See Map 29.
Size:	About 1 acre
Parking:	Neighborhood street parking
For Sports:	Basketball court, horseshoe pits
For Dining:	2 picnic tables, 2 barbecues
For Kids:	Playground
Description:	Flat with lush grass. No shade. Fenced. Under high powerlines, right next to 101.

Of Note: Location works against this park, with both traffic
noise and airport noise to contend with, but if you live
nearby, it's convenient.

Walk 5: Green Hills Park

Location: Magnolia Avenue at Ludeman Lane—easy to find.
See Map 29.

Size: About 3 acres

Parking: Neighborhood street parking

For Sports: Fitness station

For Dining: 4 game/picnic tables

For Kids: Playground

Description: Hilly, with steps cut in. Good grass and lots of new
little trees. Mostly sunny. Unfenced. Quiet. Paved
path running up and around hillside. Small.

Of Note: Another small neighborhood park.

Walk 6: Millbrae Meadows Park

Location: Access road off Helen Drive—a little hard to find. See
Map 29.

Size: About 2 acres

Parking: Neighborhood street parking

For Kids: Playground

Description: Slightly rolling, with good grass. Paved path halfway
around. Mostly sunny, with shade around the edges on
the hillside only.

Of Note: A small but pleasant park, probably most useful to
those who live nearby.

Chapter 7
San Bruno/South San Francisco

San Bruno does not allow dogs in its city parks, but has at least had the decency to set aside an area specifically for dog owners. It's a little hard to find, but well thought out, and dogs can run free within its confines.

South San Francisco, on the other hand, permits dogs in all its parks, including the huge open-space area of Sign Hill. Most parks here are large, and seem to be well used by dogs and their owners. Be alert for loose-running dogs and untended children, and be sure to keep your own dog on leash and clean up after yourselves.

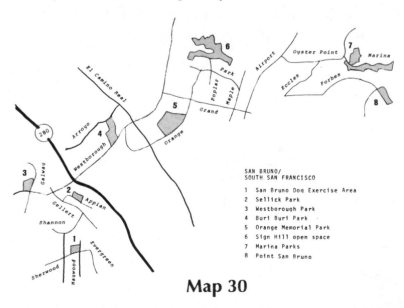

SAN BRUNO/
SOUTH SAN FRANCISCO

1   San Bruno Dog Exercise Area
2   Sellick Park
3   Westborough Park
4   Buri Buri Park
5   Orange Memorial Park
6   Sign Hill open space
7   Marina Parks
8   Point San Bruno

Map 30

Walk 1: San Bruno Dog Exercise Area

Location: Evergreen and Maywood drives—a little hard to find. See Map 30.

Size: Approximately 1½ acres, all open

Parking: In school parking lot

Description: Approaching from the direction of Highway 35 on Evergreen, turn left at Maywood and down into the school parking lot. You will pass a gate on your right before the first building. Walk through that, follow the drive, and you will reach the signed dog exercise area. Large, flat, L-shaped space, completely fenced, with a water fountain. There are pooper-scoopers and lots of plastic bags attached to the fences. There's even a bulletin board.

Of Note: This could be an example to those cities that don't want to allow dogs in their parks, of how to provide an area for dog owners. I found it quite clean and well tended, and well thought out. Bravo, San Bruno.

Walk 2: Sellick Park

Location: Appian Way off Gellert Blvd.—a little hard to find. See Map 30.

Size: 3 acres, nearly all open

Parking: Lot off Appian

For Comfort: Restrooms, with wheelchair access, clean; water fountain

For Sports: Lighted tennis court, basketball court, parcourse

For Dining: 7 picnic/game tables, 2 barbecues

For Kids: Playground

Description: Hillside sloping park with good grass. Lighted, paved path looping around. Some traffic noise from 280, but not enough to be unpleasant. Good-sized stand of trees left along one side provides shade.

Of Note: This is an appealing blend of an irregular curved shape, a gentle slope, and large trees left standing.

Walk 3: Westborough Park

Location:	Galway Drive off Westborough Blvd.—easy to find. See Map 30.
Size:	10 acres, nearly all open
Parking:	Lot off Galway
For Comfort:	Restrooms, reasonably clean; water fountain
For Sports:	Basketball court, 2 tennis courts, softball field
For Dining:	6 individual picnic tables, plus group area with 2 large barbecues under shade arbor
For Kids:	Playground
Description:	Steps cut into hillside to make flat areas, with field on top area. Paved, lighted path around park on two levels. Good blend of sun and shade. Pleasant landscaping. Quiet.
Of Note:	This park offers a good, usually cool, ramble, but there is broken glass on the path in spots, so be careful.

Walk 4: Buri Buri Park

Location:	Arroyo Drive off Junipero Serra Blvd.—easy to find the vicinity but hard to spot the park; look for the wide drive and park sign. See Map 30.
Size:	7 acres, all open
Parking:	Lot off Arroyo
For Comfort:	Restrooms, clean; water fountain
For Sports:	Basketball court, 1 lighted tennis court, softball field
For Dining:	6 picnic tables, 3 barbecues
For Kids:	Playground
Description:	Mostly flat, with nice grass. Fenced. Paved, lighted path around. Occasional very loud airplane traffic overhead. Traffic noise from Westborough.

| Of Note: | Everyone in the vicinity seems to ignore the leash law, so be alert for loose-running neighborhood dogs. Also, if you are sensitive to noise, this park may be too much for you. |

Walk 5: Orange Memorial Park

Location:	Orange Avenue—easy to find. See Map 30.
Size:	21 acres, about three-quarters open
Parking:	Various lots off Orange and Eucalyptus
For Comfort:	Restrooms, clean; water fountains
For Sports:	2 softball fields, 4 lighted tennis courts, parcourse, horseshoe pitches, bocce ball courts
For Dining:	8 picnic tables, 4 barbecues
For Kids:	2 playgrounds
Description:	Mostly flat, with good grass. Softball fields fenced off. Lots of shade. Paved, lighted paths everywhere. Bridges over concrete canal.
Of Note:	I encountered plenty of both dogs and children in this park. All in all, the dogs were under a lot better control than the children. I had to practically run away from untended children trying to pet my unfriendly dog. Yet it would have been *my* fault if anyone had gotten bit. Always keep in mind that the law will blame you and your dog if anything should happen, even if you did everything possible to avoid a confrontation.

Walk 6: Sign Hill

Location:	Poplar Avenue—a little hard to find. See Map 30.
Size:	40 acres, all open
Parking:	Neighborhood street parking

Description: This is the hill sporting the SOUTH SAN FRANCISCO—THE INDUSTRIAL CITY sign. It's in its natural state other than the sign, with plenty of weeds and burrs. There are no formal trails. There are ticks and probably the occasional rattlesnake. There's no reason you can't enjoy a walk here if you don't mind a bit of bushwhacking, but use reasonable caution.

Of Note: After a walk here, or any other natural area, be sure to check your dog for burrs and ticks. Foxtails can burrow under a dog's skin and travel, creating all sorts of havoc. Be sure to find and remove them right away.

Walk 7: Marina Parks

Location: Marina Blvd. off Oyster Point Blvd.—easy to find. See Map 30.

Size: Approximately 6 acres, mostly linear along the water

Parking: Lots along Marina

For Comfort: Public restrooms

For Dining: Several picnic tables in a meadow on the left as you approach, others tucked along the trail on the bayfront, some with barbecues

Description: An open natural area along the bay, with a paved path paralleling the water some distance back. There is public shore access near the closed fishing pier. Be prepared to pick your way over sometimes-slippery rocks. All sorts of waterbirds. Quiet.

Of Note: This is a fine walk, often cool even if it's sunny.

Walk 8: Point San Bruno

Location: Forbes Blvd. and Point San Bruno—easy to find. See Map 30.

Size: Approximately 3 acres, stretched along the water

Parking: A nightmare—there are supposedly public spaces in several of the company lots, but there are very few and they were all full

For Sports: Parcourse

Description: This is a narrow planted area with a gravel path parallel with the bay. There is access to the shore at one point, with a bit of a scramble over the rocks.

Of Note: It's a lot easier to find a parking space at the Marina Parks.

Chapter 8
Pacifica and
the San Mateo County Beaches

Pacifica means beaches, and there are plenty to choose from. Some offer walks along the clifftops or beside pools of fresh water in addition to the traditional sandy beach. The ocean should always be treated with healthy respect by all who approach it. Although Pacifica doesn't have a leash law, San Mateo County does, and anyway it's not wise to let your dog run free into the treacherous surf of the Pacific Ocean. If the two of you are investigating tidepools, be sure to keep one eye on the waves.

There are also some nonbeach parks, most of them rather idiosyncratic. The strangest is surely Sharp Park. Located in Pacifica, it's nevertheless managed by San Francisco, apparently solely for the use of its police pistol range. Fairmont is the most normal and most attractive of the parks.

Walk 1: Bean Hollow Beach

Location:	Highway 1 north of Pigeon Point Light. See Map 31.
Parking:	Lot off Highway 1
For Comfort:	Restrooms locked, portable toilets in use
For Dining:	4 picnic tables, 4 barbecues around edge of parking lot
Description:	Beach divided into two sections. Stairs down to left lead to shorter but deeper sand area, with wicked surf. Trails lead up the cliffs at the end of the beach. Stairs down to right from parking lot lead to longer sand beach with milder surf and a rocky area with some tidepools at the end.

Of Note: The leash law is well-advised here, since the surf is highly treacherous and not all dogs are naturally wary of the ocean. The rocks at the far end are nice to explore with a dog.

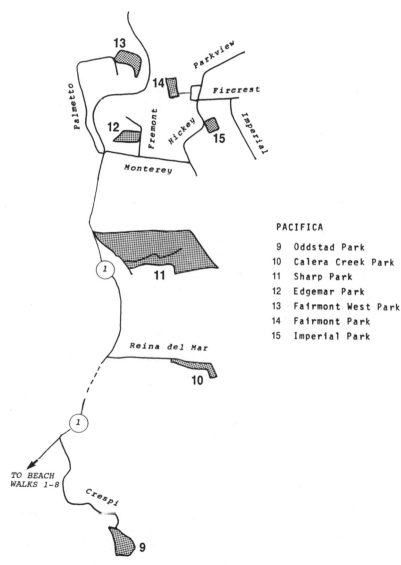

PACIFICA

9   Oddstad Park
10   Calera Creek Park
11   Sharp Park
12   Edgemar Park
13   Fairmont West Park
14   Fairmont Park
15   Imperial Park

Map 31

Walk 2: Pebble Beach

Location: Highway 1 north of Bean Hollow Beach. See Map 31.

Parking: Lot off Highway 1

Description: This beach is aptly named—there may be sand here, but it's buried in millions of pebbles, ranging from agate, jasper and jadite to pure quartz. Long steps lead down to the beach. Make a left onto the rocks for tidepools or walk across the beach to more rocks and tidepools on the far side. Don't forget to keep an eye on the surf, as people have been swept off the rocks all along this stretch of coastline.

Of Note: A prominent warning informs you it's illegal to collect the pebbles, but you can certainly pick them up and admire the many colors.

Walk 3: Pescadero Beach

Location: Highway 1 north of Pebble Beach. See Map 31.

Parking: Long lot extends along top of bluff, second lot farther north has day use and dog fees

For Comfort: Portable toilets

For Dining: 3 picnic tables, 2 barbecues

Description: The beach is not continuous. Some of the trails down are steep, some not so bad. Some beach sections are sand, some small pebbles, some larger rocks. Really huge rocks lead out into the ocean, with waves crashing against and sometimes over them. From the far end of the first parking lot you can walk down to the long sandy section of beach if you don't mind wading a shallow creek running in from the marsh. Otherwise you can park in the second lot and pay the fee.

Of Note: As the parking fee seems to indicate, the northern-most section of this beach is the nicest, with lumpy sand dunes to climb, a gentler surf, and the creek running in from the marsh. Some dogs feel safer in the creek, and their owners should share their feelings.

Walk 4: Pompano Beach

Location: Highway 1 north of Pescadero Beach. See Map 31.

Parking: Lot with car fee plus dog fee

For Comfort: Outhouses

For Dining: 8 picnic tables, 8 barbecues

Description: Long, flat sand beach with a somewhat milder surf than most of the other. Seems to be one of the most popular.

Of Note: A nice walk, but by no means a solitary one, even on a winter weekday. There's a nice trail along the top of the bluffs, where there aren't so many people.

Walk 5: San Gregorio Beach

Location: Highway 1 north of Pompano Beach. See Map 31.

Parking: Lot with car fee plus dog fee

For Comfort: Rows of portable toilets; pay phone

For Dining: 6 picnic tables, 5 barbecues

Description: Long sandy beach, even longer than it looks because you can sneak around the bluffs at what appears to be the end if you time the waves right. Several small caves under the hillside let you get out of the wind. Trail also runs across the bluff tops, but stay back from the edge as the signs warn, for the cliffs are always crumbling.

Of Note: There is a good-sized pond and stream of semi-fresh water, where dogs can enjoy a swim without having to worry about the surf.

Walk 6: Half Moon Bay State Beaches

Location: Half Moon Bay. See Map 31.

Parking: Each beach has its own parking lot, most with fees (or state parks association membership)

For Comfort: Restrooms at Dunes Beach and Harbour Beach

Description: Venice Beach is currently closed in order to improve the access.

Dunes Beach is a long sand beach with a gentler surf than many. It's a short walk down from the parking lot.

Harbour is a rough scramble down a short stretch of rocks to a long sand beach. A long breakwater protects the harbor, but walking on it is not advised, as the waves can be very dangerous.

Of Note: Both sand beaches are very appealing, but Dunes is a little safer because of its gentler surf.

Walk 7: Montara State Beach

Location: North of Half Moon Bay, at southern edge of Pacifica—easy to find. See Map 31.

Parking: Small free lot

For Comfort: Portable toilets

Description: Long, wide sand beach below sheer cliffs. Either a rough scramble down a dirt hillside, or use the stairs behind the Chart House restaurant. The surf is nasty and there's a bad undertow, so use caution.

Of Note: The sand is deep and loose until you get near the surf. Walking can be a real workout.

Walk 8: Linda Mar Beach

Location: Highway 1 north of Montara State Beach. See Map 31.

Parking: Lot with fee

Description: A *very* long beach, with rocky tidepools at the north end. You can really walk here if you go all the way up and back.

Of Note: The tidepools are very interesting.

Walk 9: Oddstad Park

Location: Crespi Drive off Highway 1—easy to find. See Map 31.

Size: About 4 acres

Parking: Upper and lower lots

For Comfort: Restrooms, water fountain

For Sports: Derelict bocce ball court

For Dining: 3 picnic tables, 2 barbecues

For Kids: Playground

Description: Hillside, mostly natural, with small, flat grass area around the upper parking lot. Sunny at the top, shady down below. Bird song is the prevalent sound. Paved road leads up and around.

Of Note: If you want to get away from the sun and wind of the beach, this park is sheltered and shady.

Walk 10: Calera Creek Park

Location: Beside Reina del Mar Avenue off Highway 1—easy to find. See Map 31.

Size: About .5 acre

Parking: Neighborhood street parking

Description: Just a shrubby median between two narrow roads, with barely a trickle of water in the bottom.

Of Note: This may be a godsend to the local small wildlife, but there's no way for a human and a dog to do anything more than look at it.

Walk 11: Sharp Park

Location: Access road off Highway 1—hard to find. See Map 31.

Size: 100 acres or more

Parking: Lots at rifle and archery ranges

Description: This is a large open-space area, mostly forested. But there doesn't appear to be any maintained access other than at the rifle and archery ranges. If you for some reason decide to bushwhack through here, be sure to stay well clear of the guns and bows and arrows.

Of Note: This park seems to be intended for use only by the local wildlife.

Walk 12: Edgemar Park

Location: Fremont Avenue off Monterey Road—a little hard to find. See Map 31.

Size: About 2 acres

Parking: Neighborhood street parking

For Dining: 4 picnic tables, 1 barbecue

For Kids: Playground

Description: Slightly rolling, with very lush grass. Dirt path looping through and around. Plenty of trees for shade in case the fog ever deserts the coast.

Of Note: This is a pleasant little park, with all rounded edges and rounded hills.

Walk 13: Fairmont West Park

Location: Palmetto at the Daly City boundary—hard to find. See Map 31.

Size: About 1.5 acres

Parking: Lot on Palmetto

For Sports: Basketball court, softball field

For Dining: 3 picnic tables, 1 barbecue

For Kids: Playground

Description: Mostly flat, with trail leading up hill to houses on Arcadia. Weedy grass on flat area. Shade under pines around edges. Unfenced. Some traffic noise from Highway 1.

Of Note: A bit hard to get to, but nice if you live around here and don't feel like going to the beach.

Walk 14: Fairmont Park

Location: Access from Parkview Circle off Hickey Blvd.—a little hard to find. See Map 31.

Size: 6.5 acres, mostly open

Parking: Lot off Parkview

For Comfort: Restrooms, reasonably clean; water fountain

For Sports: Fitness center, basketball courts, horseshoe pits, recreation building

For Dining: 7 picnic tables, 2 barbecues

For Kids: 2 playgrounds

Description: Fairly flat with very lush grass. Several open lawn areas that would be sunny if there were no fog. Paved path leading around. Very quiet. Probably a view on clear days.

Of Note: This park was fogged in even when the beaches were perfectly clear.

Walk 15: Imperial Park

Location: Access off Imperial Drive—a little hard to find. See Map 31.

Size: About .5 acre

Parking: Neighborhood street parking

Description: Really just a playground and some ice plant amid scrubby grasses. There might be a view if the fog ever clears.

Of Note: This isn't worth taking the time to find.

Chapter 9
Daly City

The city just below the "city by the bay" shares its characteristic summer fog. Parks here don't offer much shade, but that usually presents no problems as the sun is kept from sight. On those rare days when it is too hot and you want to visit a park, head for Hillside. It's the shadiest of the lot. Remember to take some sandwich bags along for cleanup, and keep your dog on leash.

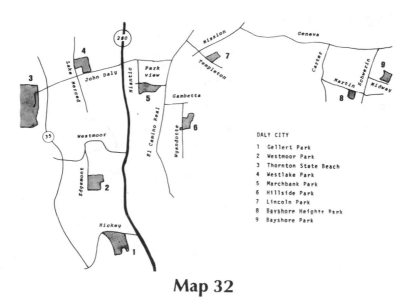

DALY CITY

1 Gellert Park
2 Westmoor Park
3 Thornton State Beach
4 Westlake Park
5 Marchbank Park
6 Hillside Park
7 Lincoln Park
8 Bayshore Heights Park
9 Bayshore Park

Map 32

Walk 1: Gellert Park

Location: Gellert and Hickey blvds.—easy to find. See Map 32.

Size: About 4 acres

Parking: Lot off Wembley

For Comfort: Restrooms, clean, wheelchair access; water fountain

For Sports: 3 tennis courts, basketball courts, handball court, volleyball courts (no nets), soccer field, lighted softball field

For Dining: Group area with 2 large barbecues under sheds

For Kids: Small playground

Description: Mostly flat grass fields. Open and sunny. No paths except stairs leading up or down to surrounding streets. Very little shade. Mostly fenced. Library and community building on property.

Of Note: If there are no sports going on, the expanse of fields is quite large. There is no shade, but the fog stays here most of the summer.

Walk 2: Westmoor Park

Location: Edgemont Drive off Westmoor Avenue—easy to find. See Map 32.

Size: About 2.5 acres

Parking: Lot off Edgemont

For Sports: Softball field, 4 tennis courts

For Kids: Small playground

Description: Fairly flat, with manicured lawn. Scattered small trees for shade. Paved path loops across. Mostly fenced. Some traffic noise.

Of Note: A nice, windswept, foggy, open park. Adjacent school grounds are off limits to dogs.

Walk 3: Thornton State Beach

Location: End of John Daly Blvd.—easy to find. See Map 32.

Description: At the moment, the access road is closed for repairs. If you want to know when this one is scheduled to reopen, or if it has, contact the state parks department.

Walk 4: Westlake Park

Location: Lake Merced Blvd.—easy to find. See Map 32.

Size: About 5 acres, hardly any open space

Parking: Lot off Lake Merced

For Sports: 4 lighted tennis courts, parcourse

For Kids: 2 playgrounds

Description: Mostly taken up by senior center, community center, a whole cluster of buildings. What open grass there is has some slope to it, but there's not much.

Of Note: This is not a park for dogs.

Walk 5: Marchbank Park

Location: North Parkview Avenue off Niantic Avenue—a little hard to find. See Map 32.

Size: About 3 acres

Parking: Neighborhood street parking

For Sports: Softball field, basketball court

For Kids: Playground

Description: Flat grass area at bottom of bowl with steps down from the road. Shade around edges. Fenced. Playground on separate upper level.

Of Note: This is not the best place to try to drive, as streets are narrow and clogged with parked cars.

Walk 6: Hillside Park

Location: Lausanne Avenue off Market Street—easy to find. See Map 32.

Size: About 5 acres

Parking: Neighborhood street parking

For Comfort: Water fountain

For Sports: 2 tennis courts, basketball court

For Dining: 1 picnic table

For Kids: Playground

Description: Sloping grass section with fine patch of shade in the middle. Hilly up one side, with dirt paths leading up the hill in several directions. One path has stairs, the other just climbs. Unfenced.

Of Note: One of Daly City's more attractive parks, cool and appealing.

Walk 7: Lincoln Park

Location: Brunswick Street off Acton Street—easy to find. See Map 32.

Size: About 2 acres

Parking: Small lot off Brunswick

For Sports: Basketball court

For Kids: Playground

Description: Rolling terrain with good grass. Mostly sunny but some small trees for shade. Unfenced. Long, narrow strip between two streets.

Of Note: A pleasant park, but be sure to keep your dog on leash and out of traffic.

Walk 8: Bayshore Heights Park

Location:	Martin Street off Carter Street—easy to find. See Map 32.
Size:	About 1.5 acres
Parking:	Small lot off Martin
For Comfort:	Restrooms, reasonably clean; water fountain
For Dining:	Group area with tables under shade arbor
For Kids:	Playground
Description:	Side-hill sloping park with manicured lawn. Paved path zigzags from one end of park to the other while climbing gradually. All sun.
Of Note:	Backs on an area of open space under high powerlines.

Walk 9: Bayshore Park

Location:	Midway Drive off Schwerin Street—a little hard to find. See Map 32.
Size:	About 1.5 acres
Parking:	Small lot on Midway
For Sports:	Softball field
For Kids:	Playground
Description:	Flat with good grass. Sunny but windy. Short paved path. Unfenced. Quiet.
Of Note:	Next to all sorts of high powerlines and a switching station. If you're concerned about the possible effects of such things, don't come here.

Dogs Are Not Welcome In

Menlo Park
Flood Park

Belmont
O'Donnell Park

Redwood City
any Redwood City park

San Carlos
any San Carlos city park

San Bruno
any San Bruno city park

Brisbane
any Brisbane city park

San Mateo County
any San Mateo County park

San Mateo County Beaches
Año Nuevo State Reserve
Gazos Creek Coastal Access
James V. Fitzgerald Marine
    Reserve

Appendix 1
Places Where You Can Really Take A Hike

San Jose
Los Alamitos-Calero Creek (currently scheduled to be expanded even farther, with trail work from McKean Road to Lake Almaden)
Santa Teresa County Park
Saratoga Creek Park
Coyote Creek County Park
Kelley Park
Penitencia Creek Park Chain

Milpitas
Murphy through Yellowstone to Sinnott Park
Peter D. Gill to Reuther Park

Santa Clara
Central Park

Los Gatos/Campbell
Los Gatos Creek Trail
Vasona Lake County Park
Belgatos Park
Novitiate Park in St. Josephs Open-Space Preserve

Sunnyvale
Baylands (County)

Cupertino
Fremont Older Open-Space Preserve

Los Altos Hills
Byrne Preserve

Mountain View
Cuesta Park

Palo Alto
Foothills Park (residents and guests only)
Foothills Open-Space Preserve
Palo Alto Baylands
Bol Park
Trails off Arastradero Road

County and Open Space
Windy Hill Open-Space Preserve
Long Ridge Open-Space Preserve
Lexington Reservoir Water Recreation Area
Uvas Reservoir
Anderson Reservoir

Pacifica
Pescadero Beach
Linda Mar Beach

South San Francisco
Sign Hill Open Space
Marina Parks

San Mateo
Laurelwood Park

Foster City
Leo J. Ryan Park

Belmont
Waterdog Park and Brooks Memorial Open Space

Menlo Park
Bayfront Park

Appendix 2
Organizations Dealing With Dogs

If you are looking for a new dog, or through some misfortune have lost your own dog, the local humane society or the animal service center is a good place to go.

Humane Society of Santa Clara Valley
2530 Lafayette Street
Santa Clara, CA
(408) 727-3383
Hours: 11–6 Mon–Fri., 10–5 Sat.

Besides housing animal control for much of Santa Clara County (although this is in the process of changing, as the Humane Society has decided not to accept the county contract), this society offers such programs as Hug-a-Pet (pet and handler visits to hospitals and nursing homes) and grief counseling for those who have suffered the death of a pet.

South County Pound
12370 Murphy Avenue
San Martin, CA
(408) 683-4186
Hours: 11–5:30 Mon.–Fri.

Palo Alto Animal Services
3281 East Bayshore Frontage Road
Palo Alto, CA
(415) 329-2671
Hours: 11–5:30 Mon.–Sat.

Covers the Palo Alto city limits only.

Peninsula Humane Society
12 Airport Blvd.
San Mateo, CA
(415) 573-3720
Hours: 11–6 Mon.–Fri., 11–5 Sat.

Covers all of San Mateo County.

There are other organizations that concern themselves with strays and placement. Many of the purebred dogs are covered by their own rescue societies. As there are a great variety of these, inquire at your local humane society or breed group if you would like to get in touch. For general pet rescue, try the following.

The Rescuers
The Animal Society of Los Gatos and Saratoga
Box 64
Los Gatos, CA 95031
(408) 354-5572

Pets in Need
585 Glenwood Avenue
Menlo Park, CA
(415) 327-5855

Nike Animal Rescue Foundation (NARF)
(408) 224-6273

If you already have a dog, or are just about to bring one into your home, you may be interested in obedience training. As I said in the Introduction, I do recommend at least basic obedience training for the benefit of both you and your dog. I cannot personally recommend a particular trainer or club, but here are several to get you started on your search.

Bay Area Dog Training
19997 Stevens Creek Blvd., Suite 6
Cupertino, CA 95014
Group or in-home obedience and behavior modification training.

Baymont Dog Training
129 Jose Figueres
San Jose, CA 95116

Companion Dog Training
10450 Creston Drive
Los Altos, CA 94024

Deep Peninsula Dog Training Club
1687 Dalehurst Avenue
Los Altos, CA 94022
Group obedience and show training.

Oz Training
5607 Makati Circle
San Jose, CA 95123
Individual or small group obedience and behavior modification training.

San Mateo Dog Training Club
1514 Lorraine Avenue
San Mateo, CA 94401

Santa Clara Dog Training Club
12366 Priscilla Lane
Los Altos Hills, CA 94022

Televet
41708 Higgins Way
Fremont, CA 94539
Individual or small group obedience and behavior modification training, plus telephone consultation at (415) 651-2381.

Town and Country Dog Training Club
1714 Hydrangea Lane
San Jose, CA 95124
Group obedience and show training.

West Valley Dog Training Club
1061 Clark Avenue
Mountain View, CA 94040

There are also several organizations that take a deeper look at the human-dog bond and interaction. The first does offer some training, but the other two are oriented toward research, and even offer grants.

Ian Dunbar
Center for Applied Animal Behavior
2140 Shattuck Avenue, Suite 2406
Berkeley, CA 94704

Latham Foundation
Latham Plaza Blvd.
Clement & Schiller Streets
Alameda, CA 94501
Information on the human-animal relationship and treatment of pets.

Delta Society
P.O. Box 1080
Renton, WA 98057-1080
Exploration of the human-animal bond.

There are also some hotlines that deal with pets, and emergency clinics for those times when your own vet may not be available. I am familiar only with the clinic in the South Bay. If you do not live in the San Jose area and would like to know the location of the nearest emergency clinic, your regular vet or local humane society should be able to supply you with that information.

Animal Poison Information
Illinois Animal Poison Information Center
1-800-548-2423 (toll-free)

Pet Loss Support Hotline
UC Davis, School for Veterinary Medicine
Human-Animal Program
(916) 752-4200

Hours: Monday through Friday, 6:30–9:30 p.m.

United Emergency Animal Clinic
1657 S. Bascom Avenue
Campbell, CA 95008
(408) 371-6252

Hours: 24 hours on weekends and holidays, 6 p.m.–8 a.m. weeknights.

There are also some groups that deal only with a specific aspect of animal medicine or dog ownership. They are listed below with a brief description of their reason for being.

American Dog Owners Association
1654 Columbia Turnpike
Castleton, NY 12033
Brings lawsuits, even providing the attorney, on behalf of individuals on dog-related issues. Very active in the defense of the American pit-bull terrier.

American Holistic Veterinary Medical Association
2214 Old Emmorton Road
Bel Air, MD 21014
Alternative medical approaches, including homeopathy, herbal medicine.

Furry Friends
Box 1593
Morgan Hill, CA 95038
Pet-assisted therapy, with members visiting hospitals and nursing homes with their pets.

National Association for Veterinary Acupuncture
1900 Sunnycrest
Fullerton, CA 92635
Promotes acupuncture as an alternative treatment.

Orthopedic Foundation for Animals
2300 Nifong Road
Columbia, MO 65201
Clearinghouse for information on orthopedic diseases, especially hip dysplasia.

Owner Handler Association of America
c/o Harry Proctor
RD 3, 89 Stagecoach Road
Lehighton, PA 18235
Breeding, training and showing of purebred dogs

R Dogs
(Responsible Dog Owners of the Golden State)
555 Capitol Mall, Suite 1500
Sacramento, CA 95814
Lobbying group for the rights of dogs and dog owners.

There is probably an organization for every breed of dog, but there are more general organizations as well. The AKC is undoubtedly the best known, but there are also the UKC and even a "breed" group for mixed-breed dogs, with a very active chapter right here in the Bay Area.

American Kennel Club
51 Madison Avenue
New York, NY 10010

Mixed Breed Dog Clubs of America
1937 Seven Pines
Creve Coeur, MO 63146

Mixed Breed Dog Club of California
P.O. Box 7374
Santa Cruz, CA 95061

United Kennel Club
100 East Kilgore Road
Kalamazoo, MI 49001

Finally, there are plenty of magazines that focus on dogs or pets in general. While the following is certainly not a complete list, it can supply you with quite a stack of interesting reading.

Animal Press
Box 2099
Lakeside, CA 92040
Covers pets in general, with lots of human interest.

Bloodlines
100 E. Kilgore Road
Kalamazoo, MI 49001
Publication of the UKC, focusing on those breeds which it recognizes and the AKC does not.

Dog Fancy
P.O. Box 6050
Mission Viejo, CA 92690
Includes both mixed-breed and purebred dogs in its coverage.

Dog World
300 W. Adams Street
Chicago, IL 60606
General articles on purebred dogs.

Front and Finish
H & S Publications, Inc.
P.O. Box 333
Galesburg, IL 61402-0333
Focuses on all aspects of obedience.

Groom & Board
207 S. Wabash Avenue
Chicago, IL 60604
Trade magazine for professional groomers and kennel operators.

Kennel Review
11331 Ventura Blvd.
Suite 301
N. Hollywood, CA 91604
News coverage for purebred breeders and exhibitors.

Off-Lead
Arner Publications, Inc.
100 Bouch Street
Rome, NY 13440
Covers dog training and obedience competition.

Pets
1300 Don Mills Road
Toronto M3B 3M8, Canada
Reports on pets in general.

Pure-Bred Dogs
51 Madison Avenue
New York, NY 10010
Publication of the American Kennel Club.

If you are interested in showing your dog, there is a publication that will
be of special interest to you, listing upcoming shows throughout the
west coast.

The Campaign Trail
P.O. Box 61689
Sunnyvale, CA 94086
(408) 739-4017

All of this information should give you plenty of ways to become more involved with your dog. There are also groups for agility, herding, flyball, and scent hurdles; talent agencies that handle dogs and other pets; and probably other groups I've never even heard of. If you have something interesting to do with dogs, please let me know about it. But by all means, spend time with your own dog and enjoy each other.